THE BROOKSIDE STORY

STORY

Shops of Every Necessary Character

LaDENE MORTON

THE History PRESS

Published by The History Press
Charleston, SC 29403
www.historypress.net

Front Cover: Brookside logo is the property of the Brookside Business Association and is used here with permission.
Back Cover: Images from the author, the *Wednesday Sun,* KCMO Public Library Missouri Valley Room and Wilborn & Associates.

First published 2010
Second printing 2011
Third printing 2012

Manufactured in the United States

ISBN 978.1.59629.300.7

Morton, LaDene.
The Brookside story : shops of every necessary character / LaDene Morton.
p. cm.
Includes bibliographical references.
ISBN 978-1-59629-300-7
1. Shopping--Missouri--Brookside--History. 2. Shopping--Missouri--Kansas City--History.
3. Brookside (Mo.)--History. I. Title.
TX336.5.M8.M67 2010
381'.1--dc22
2010034445

In memory of Deborah Cramer,
A Brooksider through and through

CONTENTS

PREFACE

I have lived, worked and played in and around the Brookside Shops for more than thirty years, the exact same time I have spent in a career working with communities—as large as regions, as small as neighborhoods—simultaneously trying to help them understand their changing world and hold on to something of their (often) more vibrant pasts. It is a paradoxical goal—the world *will* change, so how can the past hold the answer to future success? But it's a compelling question, for who wouldn't want to have the best of both worlds?

It wasn't until the mid-1990s when I finally had an office in Brookside that I began to recognize it as an amazingly enduring place. In fact, Brookside is so enduring that it is often cited as a model for what is known in the planning profession as "new urbanism," a strategy for rebuilding urban communities through a healthy mix of uses operating at a neighborhood-friendly scale. The Brookside Shops may have a standing nationally as a model, but locally it is often viewed as "quaint" and a footnote in the J.C. Nichols/Country Club District story.

That very fact—that the Brookside Shops seemed relegated to historical margins—intrigued me. Brookside predates Nichols's more famous Country Club Plaza by two years and, in no small way, was where he learned valuable lessons toward the development of the Plaza. Of course, it's also true that the Plaza is the more famous sibling, in whose shadow Brookside has always lived. Yet while both are successful, the Country Club Plaza has changed in ways that Brookside has not. Brookside still continues to serve its neighborhoods with basic services. Grocery stores, drugstores and dime stores left the Plaza years ago.

It seemed reasonable that if Brookside held any secrets for success, those secrets were multiple and likely strung throughout its history. So I began to compile the story of the Brookside Shops, hoping to learn what I might about what has enabled this unique corner of Kansas City to survive. The compilation turned out to be something akin to a scrapbook, chronicling a life through snapshots, clippings, letters and other remnants. And as with a scrapbook, the gaps in entries are their own tantalizing tales. Those gaps tell me there is more work to be done on the history of Brookside, and I look forward to doing it. But in these bits of "found" history, the answers to why Brookside has endured emerge. So do the simple stories of lives lived in a very special—and perhaps unique—place, which are reason enough to share this history of the Brookside Shops.

SOURCES AND ACKNOWLEDGEMENTS

I was privileged to receive extraordinary assistance in the research of this book from many individuals and organizations, all of whom enthusiastically shared their information and expertise. The research for this book relied heavily on their incredible resources and generosity.

Brookside Business Association. The Brookside Business Association (BBA) staff and board offered their generous support for this project from its inception and graciously opened their organizational files and archives for research. Information regarding the events, promotions, advertising campaigns and organizational issues came from these archives. The BBA and its progenitors are to be praised for their faithful stewardship of these records.

City of Kansas City, Department of City Planning and Development. Information regarding Brookside zoning ordinances and the governance of Community Improvement Districts was provided through public documents generated by the City Planning Department. Within that department, the **City of Kansas City Landmarks Commission** provided information on the location of businesses and buildings. The Commission's Historic Preservation Office has in its archives photographs taken in 1940 by the Jackson County Tax Assessor's Office. Part of a PWA project, the Assessor's Office documented all of the buildings standing within Kansas City limits at that time. These files were obtained after being discarded, so unfortunately, many individual pictures were lost. Still, the Commission is to be thanked for making this invaluable resource available.

***Kansas City Star* Archives**. The archives of the *Kansas City Star* (1991 to the present), available online through the Kansas City Public Library system, provided much of the historical detail on recent events in Brookside, particularly those concerning the changes in ownership in the last two decades.

Missouri Valley Room, Central Branch, Kansas City Public Library. Unless otherwise documented, the dates and addresses of the Brookside Shops over the years were gathered from MVR's microfilm archives of City Directories. In addition, the library's assistance with the archives of the *Kansas City Star* prior to 1991 was invaluable, as was their collection of images (several of which are included here) and their vertical files on J.C. Nichols, the Nichols Company and the Brookside and Country Club District areas.

Morningside Neighborhood Association. The association's Historic Committee, the Pathfinders, provided, through its website, its Historical Overview report, which was helpful in developing the story of the Fletcher Cowherd Company and its residential development around Brookside.

News-Press & Gazette Co., St. Joseph, Missouri. Current publishers of the *Wednesday Sun*, the contemporary of the former *Wednesday Magazine*, NP&G allowed for the reprint of images from past issues. While the copies of the *Wednesday Magazine* used for this research came from the archives of the Brookside Business Association, NP&G and the past generations of the *Wednesday Magazine* are to be commended for their work, particularly during the 1950s through the 1970s, of capturing the small and large stories in Brookside within the pages of their iconic manila-colored weekly.

Western Historical Manuscripts Collection, University of Missouri–Kansas City. WHMC is the repository of the J.C. Nichols Company Scrapbooks, an amazing compilation created by longtime executive secretary of the homes association, Faye Littleton, who, in 1954, began organizing forty years of company history, including some of the images published here, into a compendium of dozens of scrapbooks. They also maintain the texts of Mr. Nichols's many speeches and writings, from which many of the "Nichols Principles" listed in Chapter 1 were gleaned.

Wilborn & Associates. Wilborn & Associates has been capturing images of Kansas City since 1921. Several of its images are included here. In addition, photographer Chris Wilborn and his staff generously shared their archives of images for review to assist in establishing the configuration of the Brookside Shops over the years.

In addition, I am grateful to the following individuals for their willingness to spend time sharing their stories of the history and life of Brookside:

Roy and Sandy Beaty, former owners of the Book Shop in Brookside.
Sarah Douglas and Abby Fields, owners of Shop Beautiful.
Jack Fox, formerly with the J.C. Nichols Company, where he served as manager of the Brookside properties in the late 1970s and early 1980s.
George Gilchrist, managing partner, BKS Real Estate, and president of the Brookside Community Improvement District.
Dr. Jay Hodge, Hodge Family Dentistry in Brookside.
Virginia and Everett Kellogg, respectively, former director of the Brookside Business Association and owner/operator of Salon Kellogg.
Marti Lee, director, Brookside Business Association/Brookside Community Improvement District.
Carla O'Neil, manager, Roasterie Café.
Greg O'Rear, resident of the Morningside Park neighborhood, for sharing his information on the Cowherd-Built Homes.
James C. Scott, architect and planner, who offered expertise on the community development issues and architectural history of Brookside.
Sheryl White, owner, the Fiddly Fig.

Finally, a special acknowledgement and thanks to **Leon Goodhart**, who, owing to his more than sixty years' association with Brookside, proved an invaluable source of information, inspiration and support. This book would not have been possible without him.

Chapter 1

BEFORE 1920

PLANNING FOR PERMANENCE

As the twentieth century began, Kansas City was an adolescent town, a mere fifty years old, and still defining its place in the world. It had grown in fits and starts, but by 1900, Kansas City had developed the muscle of strong industry, the sinew of the nation's rails and its heart pumped the life's blood of beef and grain that fed the country. Yet despite its youth, Kansas City was remarkably well groomed. City fathers were fortunate to have in the person of George Kessler a nationally recognized landscape architect who helped fashion the city's renowned parks and boulevards system. That put Kansas City among the leading cities in the City Beautiful movement of the late 1800s, a movement that promoted landscape design and monumental architecture as a means of fostering the highest ideals within a community. This was a young idea, and fortunately for Kansas City, it was also one local young man's ideal and, ultimately, life's work.

In 1919, J.C. Nichols broke ground for the Brookside Shops on the northeast corner of Sixty-third and Brookside Boulevard. By the following spring, the first building would be occupied, though it would take ten years for Nichols to complete the last of the shops. For Nichols, however, that groundbreaking was really an end—the culmination of a decade's work of planning the Brookside Shops project. The shops themselves were only the latest phase of an expansive vision that would one day influence national residential development and become Nichols's legacy—the Country Club District.

Started in 1905, the Country Club District had become Nichols's all-consuming project. He had a vision for America's first planned subdivision to be built on a massive scale. His plan for the one thousand acres (though eventually it would grow much larger) was a residential community unlike anything before it. The first houses would be designed to attract the city's wealthiest residents and, in this way, would stabilize property values. The Country Club District would boast winding boulevards and tree-lined streets, lush parks and formal landscaping, hiking trails and community gathering places, all in an attempt to make sure that the families who moved to the Country Club District stayed in the Country Club District. What would become known as the Nichols "plan for permanence" was built on J.C.'s conviction that if a community could offer its residents everything they would want and need, build it to high standards and plan for future growth, the community would last. It was a pragmatic yet philosophical view of the world that was well ahead of its time. And no community was complete without commercial development. The Country Club District was to have, as Nichols called them, "outlying shopping centers" at its four corners. And the first to be built would be the Brookside Shops.

Almost fifteen years earlier, J.C. Nichols started realizing this vision when he built his first residential development, Bismark Place, between Forty-ninth and Fifty-first Streets just east of Main Street. He learned the potential for commercial development at the Colonial Shops he built just next to Bismark Place, at the end of the streetcar line. He was already either buying outright, or securing the rights to develop, property well to the south of Bismark Place, and he first used the term "Country Club District" in his sales promotions in 1908, after he formed the company that bore his name. Confident in his vision, in 1909 Nichols bought the piece of the old Wornall Homestead that would be the site of his Brookside Shops.

It would have taken a confident visionary to see the potential in the site. Imagine an unassuming bespectacled young man not yet thirty, standing in the middle of open fields in his tailored suit and starched white shirt, his shoes covered in dust as he walks around inspecting every particular of the property, his hat pulled low to shade his relentless view of his surroundings. At the time, the Armour family (of meatpacking fortune) operated a Hereford farm adjacent on the south. Scattered around the Nichols property on the north were a hog lot, an old dairy, a cider mill, a quarry and a minor little stream that flowed from a stock pond into Brush Creek. In the context of its time, it was an industrial area.

There was no Brookside Boulevard yet, and Sixty-third Street was only a rough macadam road leading east. Wornall Road wasn't much either, though it had grown out of a trail system that was older than the city itself,

Construction of the first Brookside shops at Sixty-third and Brookside Boulevard, 1919. A "rough macadam" road, Sixty-third Street runs in foreground. *Courtesy of the Western Historical Manuscripts Collection, KC54n77.*

a road that had in generations past led Overlanders toward the westward trails and carried both Union and Confederate troops during the Battle of Westport. A small wood-frame school—Border Star—stood on the south side of the property, a handy inducement to have nearby if you're trying to build a community. The city had just expanded its limits from Forty-ninth Street all the way to Seventy-seventh Street in this part of town, so soon the Country Club District would be enjoying city services, scant though they were at the time. As he stood there, Nichols would have inventoried what needed to be done—building new streets, improving old ones, extending the streetcar line—but he knew this place on Sixty-third Street could be grown into a crossroads of commerce.

Even as he was buying property for the shops, he sold one lot on Sixty-third Street to the City of Kansas City for construction of a new police and fire station, just a block west from where he would first build. Public safety was just the sort of amenity his clientele demanded. He made certain that the new station was unlike any built before. With an English Tudor–style façade, it looked more like a house than a public building, just as Nichols's vision required. As early as 1915, Nichols was working with nationally recognized landscape architect John Nolen on a design for the shops, borrowing from the Roland Park development in Baltimore that Nichols had seen on one of his scouting expeditions for good urban design, and which was a model for many elements of the Country Club District.

In 1914, on the brink of construction, Nichols's confidence temporarily wavered, and at one point he may have considered aborting the Brookside idea. Nichols had already lived through one major housing depression in the late 1800s that left him cautious. Now the whole world was at war, and the country's economic horizon was cloudy, to say the least. However, he had also already started to invest in Brookside. He had just installed one of his "artistically designed" filling stations for the automobiles of his future homeowners, also designed to blend in with the residential development. He held on to Nolen's plans and his own vision and waited out the war. Once the armistice was signed in 1918, he immediately moved forward with the Brookside Shops.

By this time, Nichols had been building the Country Club District for nearly fifteen years, and so far it was a success. But there had been many lessons learned along the way, including the importance of keeping in close communication with the new homeowners. One tool that served Nichols well in these early years was the *Country Club District Bulletin*. The bulletin gave J.C. the opportunity to personally communicate with residents and to reinforce the principles of responsible homeownership. And of course, always there was the chance to promote. On September 1, 1919, the headline of the bulletin read "Construction Begun on First Group of Neighborhood Shops at Sixty-Third and Brookside Boulevard."

JESSE CLYDE NICHOLS: A BRIEF BIOGRAPHY

In Kansas City's history, few men have had more influence on Kansas City's history and landscape than J.C. Nichols, and within the national real estate industry, his impact is significant and enduring. He has been the subject of several books, much scholarly research and a documentary film. The Urban Land Institute's preeminent prize for Visionaries in Urban Development bears his name. His story is richer and more detailed than can be captured here, but to understand the history of the Brookside Shops it is important to know something of how Nichols came to his philosophies about development and managing the land, for Brookside was the first large-scale area in which he tested many of his beliefs.

Jesse Clyde Nichols was born in 1880 in Olathe, Kansas, when that town was a day's ride from Kansas City. His family was middle class—his father was a farmer who also managed the local grange. Known as "Clyde" as a boy, at the age of eight J.C. started working for his father. In his teens, he earned his keep by bringing local farmers' goods to markets in Kansas City. After high school, J.C. delayed college to open a wholesale meat market downtown, earning enough to pay his way through the University of Kansas, where he enrolled in 1898. He took one summer to make a bicycle tour through Europe that left him with a profound impression of what he called "the permanent character of the cities and buildings" there. He was an ace student and, upon graduation, received a master's scholarship to Harvard. He intended to study law, but a real estate course changed that plan. The professor reportedly asked his students, "Why do the residents of England live in their houses for generations, with a profound sense of pride,

J.C. Nichols

J.C. Nichols, 1922. Photo taken as member of the Kansas City School Board. *Courtesy of the Missouri Valley Special Collections, Kansas City Public Library, Kansas City, MO.*

while in America, long-term ownership of one's home seems to indicate lack of ambition or upward mobility?" That question launched Nichols's development career.

Nichols's first attempt at development focused on the American Southwest, but the Olathe farmers who had once been customers and were now his potential investors weren't interested. When a 1903 flood in the West Bottoms of Kansas City displaced the working class, J.C. was finally able to convince those farmers that housing in Kansas City, Kansas, was worth investing in. He was right. No doubt that experience in the bottoms and the bluffs of Kansas City, Kansas, gave Nichols the chance to look across the way and see that the wealthy inhabitants of Kansas City, Missouri's Quality Hill were being displaced by encroaching industry. These were the customers Nichols and his partners set their sights on next.

The Country Club District would consume the next twenty years of Nichols's career and would be tinkered with through the rest of his life and beyond. Nichols personally searched the globe for art and architecture for his neighborhoods and shops, even as he searched for examples of good building and strong design to improve his thinking. J.C. had always been a tireless worker, an often absent yet much beloved husband and father who took pride in sharing his work with his family through Sunday drives through the district. Nichols rose to civic prominence by helping to found or serve on the boards of notable local institutions such as the University of Kansas City (now the University of Missouri–Kansas City), the Kansas City School Board, the Kansas City Art Institute, the Nelson-Atkins Museum of Art and Midwest Research Institute. He did these things not for self aggrandizement but because he saw how all these institutions were important in creating a quality place in which to live, just like a well-built house or a good road were important. His reputation made him a popular speaker across the country and earned him a major appointment to President Hoover's commission on the design of Washington, D.C. But his most far-reaching influence came from the simple act of collaborating with other major developers around the country. Working with these colleagues, he helped shape the design of Cleveland's Shaker Heights, Los Angeles's Beverly Hills and Westwood and other planned communities across the country. The 1920s is still considered a golden age of American residential development, primarily because of the influence of Nichols and his contemporaries.

Nichols continued to be actively involved in the Nichols Company until his death in 1950. The day after his death, the *Kansas City Star* ran an editorial cartoon that depicted Nichols's empty desk draped in blueprints,

1917 Nichols Company promotional postcard of J.C. Nichols and family in the car, inspecting construction at Fifty-third Street just west of Brookside Boulevard. *Courtesy of the Missouri Valley Special Collections, Kansas City Public Library, Kansas City, MO.*

with the bucolic Country Club District as the background. The caption for the illustration borrowed from the famous plaque at St. Paul's Cathedral in London, honoring its architect, Sir Christopher Wren: "If you would see his monument, look around."

THE STATION BUILDING

Nichols's decision to sell the property for the police and fire station to the City of Kansas City was more than an opportunity to quickly capitalize on his investment. He saw it as an anchor. In his residential areas, he looked for the wealthy buyers to secure the district's stability. With the Station Building, he secured the city's long-term commitment to Brookside.

The station's architectural design is so in keeping with the other Nichols-built Brookside Shops that it is commonly believed that Nichols must have had a hand in its design and perhaps even its construction. It was certainly

Country Club Police and Fire Station, circa 1911. Nichols sold the property to the city and likely influenced its design. *Courtesy of WHMC KC106n293.*

19

more handsome than any other station in town, with its leaded-glass windows, slate roof and a small fishpond in front. Structured with concrete and wood, its two stories accommodated the Police Department's Station No. 3 on the east end and the Fire Department's Station No. 29 in the center and on the west end, with sleeping quarters upstairs. There were two bays for the fire trucks and a holding cell for the miscreant. The barred windows of that cell still remain. Also remaining is the receiver for the old call box system. When an emergency happened, someone need only run to any corner and pull the handle on the red call box fixed to a light pole. In the station house, that triggered a ticker-tape printout of the call's location.

The Station Building faithfully served the Brookside area for more than sixty years, but by 1978, it was too small and antiquated to retrofit for modern equipment. The city shuttered the building and moved these stations to new facilities farther east. There was plenty of potential in the property. According to newspaper accounts, about thirty businesses expressed an interest in the building. The Nichols Company was interested, too. After all, it owned the adjacent property. But the Nichols Company's interest was not in retail—it had plenty of that. What it needed was more parking.

Miller Nichols, J.C.'s son and then president of the company, wanted to demolish the building and provide access to the parking lot behind it. Miller Nichols figured that between the influence of the Nichols Company and its dominant role as a property owner in Brookside, there would be no problem in acquiring the building. He couldn't have been more wrong. Preservationists and neighbors filled the city council chambers to prevent the demolition. Public outcry brought immediate disposal of the property to a halt. Miller Nichols tried to mount a public relations campaign to change opinions, but to no avail. The city retained control of the property, and it was put under historic protection, the only building in Brookside to be so designated.

So the city became landlord, and in 1979, the building saw new life as home to Haas Motors Limited, then as the Brookside Savings Bank and then Roosevelt Bank. In 1994, tired of serving as landlord, the city put the property up for auction. By then, there were only two bids. One was the Nichols Company, which lost. In May 1995, the property was purchased by the owners of the Fiddly Fig, a longtime Brookside plant and flower shop. The Station Building remains the only Brookside property north of Sixty-third Street never to be owned by the Nichols Company.

Catalogue: The Nichols Principles

J.C. Nichols wrote and spoke extensively of his development philosophy. He was among the first to use the term "community building" to describe development and is said to have authored the first issue of the Urban Land Institute's publication, *The Community Builders Handbook.* He was a firm believer in sharing these lessons for the benefit of all rather than keeping them as trade secrets. Taken from his speeches and writings, the following quotes provide a representative sampling of his principles for development:

- "[It has not] been realized that the great instability and rapid shifts in the character and make-up of our urban areas have created a tremendous deficit in terms of obsolescence, loss of taxable values and spread of decadence and blight estimated at several billion dollars annually. The [answer] to this problem is not, as advocated by some, to continue to tear down and rebuild every twenty-five to thirty-five years, but rather to build enduring values. To do this we must think in terms of generations, not decades."

1917 postcard of Brookside Boulevard, facing north from Fifty-fourth Street, with the streetcar line and the brook for which Brookside is named on the right. *Courtesy of the Missouri Valley Special Collections, Kansas City Public Library, Kansas City, MO.*

- "[The] suburban shopping center customer expects and demands more freedom and less [*sic*] restrictions and regulations than he will willingly accept in the downtown central business district. He, or usually she, wishes to feel free to bring the baby, to come on a bicycle, or in shorts, house dress or other informal attire. She wishes to be able to visit with friends on the street or in the shop, take more time for lunch, park her car as she wishes…It is a natural outcome of the neighborhood environment and one of the reasons why neighborhood centers are becoming increasingly popular. Every effort should be made by the developer to promote this atmosphere."

- "American cities have a great opportunity in this growth of outlying shopping centers. It is possible to make them distinctive and appealing in appearance, individualistic and attractive in design and layout, affording character and color to the general appearance of the city. Cleanliness and good order, a reasonable uniformity and harmony of design, height and elevation, will go far to make our American cities more attractive, more appealing and more of unquestioned value to the people that live in these cities. Out of this order and cleanliness will come a practical beauty of great intangible value upon the spirit, patriotism and well being of any community."

- "Here are the assurances we must give future generations. That children can be born, reared, and still live in the neighborhood of their forefathers. That the home, the most precious possession in life— the real heritage of a free people—will have permanent value, and desirable, healthful and inspiring surroundings for many generations… where homes will grow old graciously."

- "Are we building our towns and cities monotonously alike, or are we accentuating their particular characteristic features and preserving their objects of natural beauty, scenic value and historic interest? Let us as realtors create order and beauty that will grapple the hearts and love of our people and inspire them to build for permanence. Let us not forget that good residential morale is as important as army morale in time of war. Let us look beyond our downtown areas, our own sub-divisions, our own particular parts of a city. Let us be citywide minded, suburban minded, and trade territory-minded in our study of future needs. Whether our cities are physically bad or physically good is largely our responsibility."

Chapter 2

THE 1920S

"SHOPS OF EVERY NECESSARY CHARACTER"

In the Roaring Twenties, Kansas City took a back seat to no other city in terms of its reputation as a wide-open town. It was all there, from the infamous political corruption of Boss Tom Pendergast to the innovative jazz stylings of Bennie Moten. At Seventy-fifth Street and Prospect Avenue, the new Fairyland Park offered a roaring new roller coaster, and just down the road at Ninety-fifth and Holmes Streets, the new Kansas City Speedway, a racetrack with a board racing surface, accommodated fifty thousand stupefied spectators witnessing cars roar by at over one hundred miles per hour.

But sin and speed weren't the only things that roared in the twenties, and Kansas City witnessed that too. Kansas City factories were producing at rates comparable to big manufacturing centers like Pittsburgh and Detroit. Adding to that, the immigrants who had arrived in waves the decade before were starting businesses and adding to local economies. Their hard work was rewarded with entrance to the middle class, the largest growing sector of the population. Radio was king, and the magazine industry exploded. Millions of listeners and readers were enticed with advertising for products that, they were assured, no home would be complete without. In the Country Club District, where abundance abounded, the brand-new Brookside Shops were poised to take advantage of it all.

In his announcement of the Brookside Shops' opening, J.C. Nichols demonstrated the same thorough approach to commercial development that he had to residential. Everything about the shops was thought out carefully, with only one purpose in mind: community stability. In describing the nature of the shops, Nichols wrote in the *District Bulletin*:

Illustration of the planned Brookside Building at Sixty-third Street and Brookside Boulevard, as promoted to the neighborhoods in Nichols's self-published *Country Club District Bulletin*, 1919. *Courtesy of WHMC KC54n76.*

We have compiled a list of more than forty enterprises, which, we believe will in time be needed and add greatly to the convenience and economy of the people living in the [district]. *Realizing the increasing difficulty, particular for the women in the District, in reaching the stores of the downtown's congested business streets, we plan to eventually provide appropriate and architecturally attractive buildings for shops of every necessary character.*

Sited on the northeast corner of Brookside Boulevard and Sixty-third Street, the English Tudor–style Brookside Building, with its half timbers and slate roof, would have presented a formidable figure in the open space in which it sat. It cost $75,000 to build, a considerable sum of money then, enough to ensure that this building was of the same quality as Nichols's homes. The building was an innovation in its time. Playing against convention, it incorporated office space on the second floor, not the living space apartments typically housing the shop owner's family. Another feature was even more of a departure. A space that would come to be called "Community Hall" took the upper floor of the building's north wing. For the next twenty years, the hall provided meeting space for the neighborhood associations, for social organizations like the Country Club Masonic Lodge #655 and for dance and music instruction. For a while, it was also the temporary home of several denominations while they built new facilities in the neighborhood, including Country Club Congregational Church, Brookside Methodist Church and Nichols's own church, Country Club Christian Church. Wisely, Nichols saw the Community Hall as another way to keep the members of the community connected to the area and one another.

Interior of the Community Hall on the second floor of the Brookside Building. It was used by groups like the Conservatory of Music and the Order of the Eastern Star. *Courtesy of WHMC KC54n663.*

As to the retail shops, Nichols believed he knew what the district would want, but he was smart enough to listen to his customers. "We will greatly appreciate," the *Bulletin*'s announcement concluded, "the suggestion of any owner as to the need of any particular kind of store or enterprise, or the name of any firm or individual especially fitted to operate in such an establishment in the Country Club District." Why risk losing business because of past loyalties or the entrenched shopping patterns of the residents? J.C. Nichols was relocating the city's upper class, and he was willing to relocate their favorite merchants, too, if it drew people to the district.

There are no apparent records of which of those early shops were handpicked by Nichols or which were referred by residents. But together they presented a pleasing mix of convenient necessities and upper-class niceties. Public directories of the time indicate that Drummond Cleaners was the first business to move in, in 1919. Five other businesses are listed there that first year. Mayme T. Keller operated an "art needlework" shop on the north end. Next door was Loretta Moore's Brookside Children's Shop. Then stood Drummond Cleaners, and just south of it was the millinery shop of Carrie Graham. The next shop belonged to Antoinette Kauffman, listed as providing "art goods." In the large space on the south end, with a view to both Brookside Boulevard and Sixty-third Street, was A. Weber, Meat & Provisions Company, Brookside's first grocer. With these first tenants, Nichols had a good start on gathering everything the Country Club District families would want.

No time was lost in moving forward. A few tenants lasted only that first year but were quickly replaced. Nichols started to expand eastward along Sixty-third Street. Logically, he focused on the area closest to the Station Building. Nichols enticed the garage on the south side of Sixty-third Street and Baltimore Avenue with the promise of a newer facility on the north, just west of the fire station. When it moved, the business changed its name to the Brookside Garage. Like the Station Building, the garage was set back from the street slightly more than the other storefronts, both to accommodate a driveway and to help an otherwise unsightly use blend into the background. It boasted two stories, with the Sixty-third Street side providing the filling station service. The lower level, accessed at grade from the north, accommodated forty-five cars in the garage area. Once again, Nichols used the *Country Club District Bulletin* to announce the new garage, along with the names and credentials of the gentlemen operating the station. C.F. Cole was introduced as "having lived in the District for the last six years," and G.J. Smith, the piece offered, "for fifteen years has been master mechanic for the Kansas City Railways Company."

The rapid pace of Nichols's construction, already underway and planned out for the next ten years, suggested an interesting method of construction efficiency. On land on the south side of Sixty-second Terrace between Main Street and Brookside Plaza, Nichols built a planing mill. The mill provided finished lumber for the construction of the new commercial buildings and their interior finishes. The planing mill occupied that location from 1921 to 1949. Over time, the Nichols Company developed a number of similar service buildings for painters, plumbers, electricians and landscaping at least, housed around his various commercial properties. This gave tenants quick access to maintenance and made changes to the interior finishes easy when Nichols had to accommodate a new tenant.

In the Brookside Building's Community Hall, the neighborhood was settling in. The hall housed three dance schools and, from 1922 to 1930, the Kansas City Conservatory of Music. It was also home for a brief while to the Country Club Day & Nursery School. Five medical professionals (three doctors, one dentist and an orthodontist) moved into the office suites. At

Interior of the lumber planing mill of the Nichols Company, on-site in Brookside for construction of shops and, later, tenant finishes. The mill operated from 1921 to 1949. *Courtesy of Wilborn & Associates.*

street level, P.J. Mason's Brookside Pharmacy replaced the grocer on the corner, but another grocer, Bacher & Cunningham, moved in next door in 1926 and would operate there for twenty-five years. Otherwise during that five-year period, a stream of photography studios, gift shops, beauty parlors, milliners and dressmakers moved in and out of the retail space, few lasting more than a year or two.

In 1922, the Nichols Company began construction of the Country Club Plaza, just fifteen blocks north of Brookside. This development was always planned to be a regional, rather than neighborhood, shopping center. J.C. Nichols would use the lessons and practices from Brookside in designing and managing the Plaza, but he would never again devote singular attention to the development of the Brookside Shops. Fortunately, he had built a strong company with capable men who embraced his philosophy. Under their guidance, throughout the rest of J.C. Nichols's life, the Brookside Shops were managed and maintained to Nichols's high standards.

From the outset, Nichols learned lessons from his Brookside experience. Over that first decade, he lost most of the medical professionals he had courted as tenants, but in their stead came contractors and builders, reflective of the robust building activity of the era. One contractor, Harry Smith, remained in Brookside for the next fifty years. At street level, the constant change in tenants taught Nichols how to change the interior space, to combine two small spaces into one large one or subdivide larger spaces. This was a tactic he employed to relocate one less valuable tenant so that he could lease space to the popular Robinson Shoe Company in 1927.

In 1925, the Nichols Company started filling out its next development phase on Sixty-third Street. The U.S. Postal Service opened the Country Club Station in its present location at 108 West Sixty-third, making it the oldest tenant in Brookside to remain in the same space. Continuing west, Nichols built the remaining shops to the corner of Sixty-third Street and Brookside Plaza. Now the Brookside Shops could boast an interior decorator, a hardware store, another grocery and its first restaurant. The next year, Nichols finished this phase by building north onto Brookside Plaza. It was known as Wyandotte Street originally, and businesses would sometimes be listed at a Wyandotte address long after the name had been changed. This stretch of retail, across from the streetcar stop, would draw some of Brookside's most stable tenants of the period, including the Old Colony Book Shop (1926–68), Sheldon & Sheldon Orthodontists (1926–50) and E.C. Deffenbaugh, dentist (1926–43).

By the end of the 1920s, the Nichols Company had finished the first two phases of its Brookside Shops. Its property extended on the north side of Sixty-third Street from Main Street all the way to Brookside Boulevard and included more than 100,000 square feet of rentable space. It had initiated the final phase, west of Brookside Boulevard on Sixty-third Street and would complete it the following year. The company might have some trouble stabilizing its tenant base, but it had no trouble finding tenants. It was early 1929, and the world's economy continued to expand. The future looked rosy, at least for a while.

THE COUNTRY CLUB DISTRICT NEIGHBORHOODS

Throughout his lifetime, J.C. Nichols was responsible for the development of some forty subdivisions now considered the Country Club District neighborhoods. The Nichols Company continued to develop areas long after

J.C.'s death, but the following list provides a general chronology of those that happened under Nichols's oversight. The dates generally represent when the subdivision was first platted. It many cases, the plats were filed prior to Nichols's ownership or development control or long in advance of actual construction. Subdivisions are in Missouri unless otherwise noted. With the exception of Crestwood, all Country Club District neighborhoods are west of present-day Brookside Boulevard, which did not exist until 1914. Plat lines on the eastern border generally followed the old streetcar line, now known as the "Trolley Track Trail."

1905—Bismark Place

1907—Rockhill Place, Rockhill Park and Rockhill Park Extension

1908— Country Side and Country Side Extension. *Also this year, J.C. Nichols first establishes his real estate company and begins using the term "Country Club District" in his sales promotions.*

1909—Rockhill Heights and Sunset Hill

1910—Country Club Ridge and Wornall Homestead. *The Wornall Homestead property includes the first piece of what becomes the Brookside Shops area.*

1911—Bowling Green, Country Club Heights and Country Club Plaza. *The city's annexation of the Country Club District property, begun two years earlier but challenged in court, is also completed, and city limits in this part of town are extended from Forty-ninth Street to Seventy-seventh Street.*

1912—Country Club District (a subdivision within the larger district) and Mission Hills. *Morningside Park, adjacent to the Brookside Shops but not a Nichols subdivision, is platted.*

1913—Westwood Park (Kansas) and Wornall Manor

1914—South Country Side

1917—Hampstead Gardens and Greenway Fields

1919—*Construction of the Brookside Shops begins.*

1920—First Crestwood subdivision lots are offered.

1922—Suncrest, Armour Hills and Stratford Gardens

1923—Armour Fields. *Also this year, the first building of the Country Club Plaza is occupied.*

1925—Romanelli Gardens and Indian Hills. *Planning for the Romanelli Shops begins.*

1926—Meyer Circle and Fieldston

1927—Loma Linda and Oak-Meyer Gardens

1930—Armour Hills Gardens

1935—Sagamore Hills

1937—Mission Woods (Kansas)
1938—Fairway (Kansas)
1940—Fieldston Hill (Kansas)
1941—Prairie Village subdivisions, which eventually will include Prairie
Hills, Prairie Village, Prairie Fields, Prairie Ridge and Corinth Hills (Kansas)
1946—Romanelli West

COWHERD-BUILT HOMES

J.C. Nichols was not the only residential developer working in the area. Others were building homes to the south and east of Brookside. Even within the Country Club District, J.C. Nichols sold property to individual builders or managed the construction for other investors. He could do so without fear of losing the quality he had established. If the market ceased to demand that standard, the deed restrictions he had in place would ensure it. Besides, most developers, eager to build comparable housing, would often fold Nichols's deed restriction format into their developments and, not infrequently, blend their houses into Nichols's existing neighborhood associations.

Working directly east of the Country Club District was Earl Hallar, and E.J. Sweeney was building farther south at Eighty-fifth Street and Wornall Road. Napoleon Dible built to the south and east as well but used a different model to produce smaller (though still quality) homes for more modest incomes. But arguably the most distinguished and successful of these developers was Fletcher Cowherd, with his Morningside Park subdivision. While today's Morningside neighborhood covers a larger area, Cowherd's Morningside Park covered the blocks directly north and east of Brookside, between Fifty-ninth and Sixty-second Streets.

Fletcher Cowherd was of the generation before Nichols and had already attained status locally as president of the Safety Federal Savings and Loan Association. He was president of the Real Estate Board of Kansas City when J.C. Nichols was merely the chair of its Street Maintenance Committee. Cowherd was twenty when he came to Kansas City in 1879, and claimed to have been on a train robbed by Jesse and Frank James. Cowherd and Kansas City had matured together.

Despite their differences in age, Cowherd and Nichols shared a philosophy. Cowherd had also spent time in Europe and was struck by the careful planning, physical beauty and permanence of Old World cities. He understood, too, the wisdom of catering to the high-income client first. In

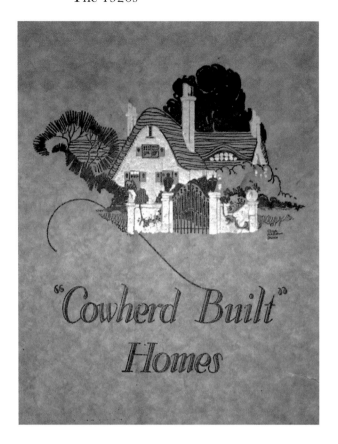

Cover of the Fletcher Cowherd Company's brochure for homes in the Morningside Park neighborhood. *Courtesy of Greg O'Rear and John Simonson.*

this regard, Morningside Park's grandest homes line Morningside Drive, but surrounding it on all sides are slightly more modest homes that blend well into the adjacent neighborhoods. The crown jewel of the Morningside Park development was the house built for Cowherd's son, Fletcher Cowherd Jr., a partner with his father in the Fletcher Cowherd Company. At 6140 Morningside Drive, the house was only a short walk to the sales office that sat beside the tracks at the west end of Sixty-first Street, near the Fifty-ninth and Brookside Boulevard shops (later moved to Sixty-second and Oak).

"'Cowherd-Built' Homes" was the brand the company gave itself, along with its motto, "The Standard of Value." The Cowherds hired nationally known architects to design their homes and, in a smaller geography, presented the same architectural vernaculars as the Nichols Company. Its brochures were a stylistic triumph, integrating photos of finished homes (complete with the names of the architect and the fortunate new homeowner) with detailed illustrations of designs in the works. The pages are replete with rich language that simultaneously extols the intrinsic virtues of the Cowherd-Built home and heralds the unparalleled success of the company. In a brochure published in 1926, in a column titled "Attainment Through Faith," the marketing copy establishes the Cowherd Company's confidence in its ability to build superior housing as the key to its success. The copy goes on to say, "The possession of such resolute faith is a priceless asset to the individual or organization engaged in any effort that entails creative effort. It is the impelling force that leads to greater attainment." Clearly, the homebuilding business of the 1920s was driven by grander ideals than at any time since.

Fletcher Cowherd was a highly successful man in multiple fields, but his life was in many ways difficult. He had married in 1886. Fletcher Jr. was his only child—he had lost another son in infancy. His wife died in 1903, as did his brother. Fletcher Jr. died suddenly of pneumonia in 1927 at the young age of forty. Fletcher Cowherd Sr. married a second time in 1935 and lived until the age of ninety-four. While the housing he constructed ranges over many blocks of the neighborhoods east of the Brookside Shops, in Morningside Park he built a lasting legacy.

CATALOGUE: A RETAIL MENU

As with all other details, J.C. Nichols developed a strong opinion on the mix of necessary commercial tenants. Over the years, he came up with a recommended menu of businesses that should be included in any successful center. The list began with ten types recommended for small centers, another ten to be added as the center grew to medium size and a final ten for when it reached its maximum size. As a medium-sized center, the following is the list that would have applied to Brookside, the original tenants who would have filled that role and the year in which they were first tenants. That so many were long-term tenants says much about the wisdom of J.C. Nichols's model.

- Drugstore—P.J. Mason's Brookside Pharmacy, 6249 Brookside Boulevard, 1922.
- Cash and Carry Grocery—A. Weber Meats & Provisions, 6245 Brookside Boulevard, 1920. *A cash and carry grocery store was one that served other grocery retailers or foodservice businesses such as restaurants.*
- Service Grocery—Piggly Wiggly, 120 West Sixty-third Street, 1925. *Piggly Wiggly was the first national service grocer. Service grocers were self-serve,*

Interior of Piggly Wiggly at 20 West Sixty-third Street, circa 1925. An innovation at the time, Piggly Wiggly was the first chain of self-service groceries. *Courtesy of Wilborn & Associates.*

like modern groceries, as opposed to stores where clerks filled the customers' orders from shelves. The Brookside store was "Piggly Wiggly No. 23."

- Beauty Parlor—Fern Rush's Brookside Beauty Shop, 6241 Brookside Boulevard, 1922. *One of fewer than two dozen beauty shops in the entire city at the time, the Brookside Beauty Shop would operate until 1975.*
- Filling Station—Brookside Standard Station, 6223 Brookside Boulevard, 1918. *This was the first building Nichols built in Brookside, and it would remain a Brookside presence until the 1990s.*
- Bakery—Manor Baking Company No. 2, 126 West Sixty-third Street, 1927.
- Shoe Repair—Brookside Shoe Shop, 6249 Brookside Plaza, 1927.
- Cleaners, Dyers and Laundry—Drummond Cleaners, 6237 Brookside Boulevard, 1919. *Though under different ownership today, Drummond Cleaners, now at 6328 Brookside Plaza, is the oldest Brookside tenant.*
- Barbershop—O.D. Stewart, 6247 Brookside Plaza, 1926.

- Milliner—Shadwell Shop, 128 West Sixty-third Street, 1927. *The Shadwell Shop operated until 1960.*
- Radio and Electrical Shop—Country Club Electric Shop, 6241 Brookside Plaza, 1927. *Over the years, the Country Club Electric Shop would change its names to reflect the times but would remain a Brookside staple until 1992.*
- Children's Clothing—Brookside Children's Clothing, 6231 Brookside Boulevard, 1920.
- Gift Shop—Marie Antoinette Gifts, 6241 Brookside Boulevard, 1922.
- Ice Cream, Candy and Nut Shop—Katydid Candy Co., 6241 Brookside Boulevard, 1927.
- Dress and Lingerie Shop—Bruton's Dry Goods, 112 West Sixty-third Street, 1925. *Bruton's operated until 1955.*

The following four store types, still part of the Nichols model, were not present in Brookside until after the 1920s:
- Florist—*The first business identified as a florist was Mrs. Otto Peed's, 310 West Sixty-third Street, in 1931. After that, the Peed family operated a florist (and for a while a catering service) in the Brookside Shops until 1978.*
- Liquor Store—*Because of Prohibition, there would have been no liquor store in Nichols's original tenant plan for Brookside. In fact, it would be 1944 before Michael Berbigilia closed the grocery he had operated for four years at 105 West Sixty-third Street to open a liquor store at 21 West Sixty-third Street, where it remains today as the only full-service liquor store in Brookside's history.*
- Haberdashery—*This has been the most difficult type of business on the list to sustain in the Brookside Shops. The first was Shapiro's Men's and Boys' Shop, 326 West Sixty-third Street, 1937–62. The only other two exclusively men's shops to last more than a year are the Jack Norman Men's Shop (1953–66) and Mister Guy (1967–76), both operating out of 6304–08 Brookside Plaza.*
- Variety Store—*The first variety store in Brookside was Ben Franklin, 314 West Sixty-third Street, in 1941. It has been the only site for a variety store in Brookside, through four different iterations, to today's the New Dime Store.*

Chapter 3

THE 1930S

An Investment Pays Off

The freewheeling 1920s made the Depression of the 1930s seem all the more stark. But an ironic stroke of fortune positioned Kansas City better than most. The city's "savior" was notorious political boss Tom Pendergast. Publicly, he owned a concrete business, though it was no secret he controlled the city from the city manager on down. Whether you needed a job or a house—and many did in these hard times—or a favor more unsavory, Pendergast was the man to see. It is no wonder, then, that one of his largest gambits in cronyism was to ensure the city pass a $40 million bond issue to build what would be some of the city's grandest art deco-era landmarks, including City Hall, the Jackson County Courthouse and Municipal Auditorium. Whether by luck or design, he managed to have the commitment in place before the stock market crashed. Of course, his concrete business would benefit, though it meant an indescribable abuse of public funds. But jobs were created, and some of the improvements were sorely needed. The projects kept Kansas City on economic life support.

Despite their affluence, the Country Club District residents were not immune to the crash of 1929. Among the descendants of those who lived there during the Great Depression, there are stories of boarders quietly taken in so mortgage payments could be met, or small businesses secretly run from the home, to bring in a few dollars more. There was crime, too. Two of the city's most notorious kidnappings involved Country Club District residents—women's clothing maven Nell Donnelly (Crestwood) and Mary McElroy, the daughter of City Manager H.E. McElroy (Sunset Hill). The Nichols Company itself laid many people off and eliminated amenities in the district, like sponsoring the gardening contests and publishing the *Country Club District Bulletin*. Instead, the company focused on maintaining those features most important to the district's success, and that included its commercial operations. Fortunately, Nichols had invested in those relationships from the beginning, and now he was, no doubt, glad he had.

In 1919, even as he was breaking ground on the Brookside Building, J.C. Nichols attended a conference of the national realtors' association. Among his peers, Nichols had a sterling reputation. The Country Club District was emerging nationally as a model for development, so when Nichols spoke, the industry listened. But this time, the presentation he made in the closing hours of the conference did not interest his colleagues. They were homebuilders, and Nichols suddenly wanted to talk retail. He announced to the gathering that he was adopting an unprecedented lease arrangement with his retail tenants. Instead of a flat rate, he would be charging them based on their sales, a practice that would come to be known as "the percentage lease." His only experience with flat rate leases had been the Colonial Shops. The Brookside Shops' tenants would be the first under this innovative approach.

No doubt the Colonial Shops had shown Nichols that retail income would rise as the housing development grew. In addition, lessons taken from the 1890s' housing bust may have left Nichols with a sense of wariness about too heavily relying on residential development to sustain his long-term vision for the district. Diversifying into retail would spread his investment risk. Most importantly in his view, Nichols saw that the percentage lease would help forge a mutually beneficial relationship between the Nichols Company as landlord and its retail tenants. Nichols had used that type of cooperation between the district residents and the company, and he knew he could do the same with the merchants.

A decade later, his innovative thinking was paying off. Through the Depression, whatever stability the Brookside Shops maintained is likely in large part due to Nichols's innovative percentage lease arrangement. True, his income dropped as his merchants' sales fell, but because of it, Nichols was invested in their success. With the economy decimated, there wasn't a backlog of tenants to replace them. Besides, Nichols was already attracting the best of what was available. In this regard, his only competition was himself, with the Country Club Plaza. Nichols is reported to have let even the base rents go if he thought the business was something the community needed. But Nichols managed his tenants like any other asset. If he thought one would do better in another of his commercial spaces, he would move them. He had built his buildings so it was easy to tear down interior walls and create just the right configuration in just the right location for each tenant.

When first built, storefronts opened to Brookside Boulevard on the east side. Later, the corner drugstores expanded into this space, and windows and doors were closed up. *Courtesy of the Brookside Business Association.*

Despite the hard times of the 1930s, this was Brookside's golden age of development. During this decade, the Nichols Company initiated the last major expansion of the Tudor-themed buildings, on the north side of Sixty-third Street, between Brookside Boulevard and Wornall Road. Most of what ultimately was built in this stretch was ready and leased by mid-1930, and it would be another ten years before the company built anything else in Brookside. But by now, J.C. was not alone in Brookside. Development was beginning on the south side of Sixty-third Street, in a very big way.

Harry Jacobs, Brookside's Southside Developer

Harry Jacobs had only been in Kansas City since 1910. He had come from Hungary a year before that, emigrating with his parents. After a brief stint in a New York factory, he was convinced there was another America. He came to Kansas City alone, made friends within the local Jewish community and soon married and started a family. First he worked selling clothing and

Harry Jacobs, the largest developer of Brookside Shops property on the south side of Sixty-third Street. *Courtesy of Leon Jacobs & family.*

then insurance. He worked hard, lived a frugal life and managed, by the time he reached thirty, to have bought his first property. He built a few homes, mostly one at a time, moving his young family to each one as it was completed, using it as a show home and, when it sold, moving to the next. He did well but was not extravagant in his dealings and, most importantly to him, succeeded solely on his own efforts.

Harry had prior real estate dealings with the Groves family, who owned a block of property on the south side of Sixty-third Street, along what was then Wyandotte Street. In the early '20s, Harry saw the potential in that property, but it took him until 1932 to convince the Groves to sell. He bought most of the property on the east side of the street and the north end of the west side. On that spot, there was an existing tenant, but Jacobs saw an opportunity in a promising new company. He quickly leased the space to the Stover Candy Company, now Russell Stover Candies. That company built one of its first retail outlets, known then as Mrs. Stover's Bungalow Candies. The Kansas City version was art deco in design, though nationally, Stover's standard shop looked like a small white cottage. Next door, the Country Club Dairy built a soda fountain and called it the Oasis. These businesses were there through the mid-'40s.

For the east side, Harry Jacobs had his own vision. It might have been slightly smaller than J.C. Nichols's vision, but it was ambitious in its own way and, like Nichols's, was based on giving the community what it wanted. Harry Jacobs would build something that looked very much like the Nichols buildings, with retail space on the ground level and offices above. But the building would be named for its most notable tenant. It would be the

This page: 1940 city survey photos of Harry Jacobs's first Brookside tenants: Mrs. Stover's Bungalow Candies (precursor to Russell Stover Candies), *top*, and the Country Club Oasis, *bottom*. *Courtesy of the Kansas City (MO) Landmarks Commission.*

Brookside Theatre Building, housing a small but ornate movie palace, so fashionable in those days. The Brookside Theatre Building, with its brightly lit rooftop sign, was no doubt aesthetically everything J.C. Nichols didn't want for the Brookside Shops—garish and obtrusive. But it accomplished something important—the word "Brookside" was clearly visible to anybody passing through the area.

The Brookside Theatre Building would be a local landmark until it was destroyed by fire in 1978. But when it was new, the Theatre Building more than doubled the number of tenants in Brookside, particularly in terms of offices. Jacobs started planning for the building from the early 1930s, but it would be 1937 before the first tenants moved in. Upstairs tenants were a mix of dentists and beauticians at first. Downstairs were a dry goods store and the Oviatt Shoe Store, which would be a tenant until 1960.

Harry Jacobs would go on to develop other commercial properties, principally in the Missouri-side suburbs of Raytown and Gladstone. But Brookside would always be his business home. One of his sons, Leon Jacobs, became his partner in the business. His other son, Dr. Morton Jacobs, a well-respected Kansas City psychiatrist, housed his practice in his father's properties for thirty-five years. As of 2010, the company now known as Jacobs Properties still owns and manages property in Brookside as a family-run business.

MINDING THE STORES: THE BROOKSIDE BUSINESS ASSOCIATION

Just as he had with his Country Club District neighborhoods, J.C. Nichols formed merchants' associations for his commercial tenants. The motivation and the principles were the same as they had been for the homeowners—good communication intended to keep everyone invested in the district's success. Nichols formed the first merchants' group less than a year after Brookside opened, in December 1920. Originally it was known as the Country Club District Merchants' Association and included both the Brookside merchants and those at the Colonial Shops at Fifty-first and Oak Streets. When the Crestwood Shops opened in 1922, they were included as well. The Plaza Merchants Association, formed in 1923, was always a separate entity, though from time to time the Nichols Company would convene the groups to discuss promotions and other matters of common interest.

By the 1930s, Brookside was emerging as a separate entity. The new group called itself the "Sixty-third and Brookside Merchants Association," according to its 1937 membership directory (thought to be the organization's first published directory). It also referred to the district as the "Brookside Shopping Centre," the British variant spelling perhaps a nod to Brookside's faux-Tudor look. The directory included seventy-two businesses, all but two of which are within the boundaries of the current district, although no professional tenants—no doctors, dentists or attorneys. However, in the back of the book alongside the advertising, a small notice read, "In addition to the shops listed in this Directory, the following professional services may be found at 63rd & Brookside: Dentists, Orthodontists, Pediatricians, Physician and Surgeon, Osteopathic Physician." At the time, advertising by professionals was very rare.

In 1939, the organization filed for its pro forma decree of incorporation with the Jackson County Circuit Court, but this time under the name "63rd & Brookside Business Association." There is no record of what, if anything, prompted Brookside's break from the other Country Club District commercial areas. Most likely this organizational independence was simply the next logical step in each commercial area's own growth.

There are few records of Brookside's organizational life over the next twenty years or so. There are accounts of annual dinners for members and of course plenty of clippings on promotions and events, as well as a few scattered letters pertaining to tenant-related matters. But there is no information about how the organization functioned day-to-day, presumably because the Nichols Company handled most matters. Then, in 1958, the Brookside Merchants Association (as it called itself then) hired its first staff person. Bea Miller Mann had been an employee of Brookside's own Crick Camera for several years before she took on the official title of executive secretary for Brookside. For the first three years, Mrs. Mann worked out of Harry Jacobs's real estate office doing the relatively minor bookkeeping and correspondence duties the job required. In 1961, the association formally leased space from Jacobs and had its first office in the basement at 6314 Brookside Plaza.

In those early days, the *Wednesday Magazine* ran a feature that Bea herself would write each week, called "Merchant of the Week." The *Wednesday* would always have a special two-page layout for Brookside (as it would for other areas such as Waldo, the Landing and Prairie Village), and the "Merchant of the Week," piece would be included in that section. The *Wednesday* wrote its own profile of Bea Mann one week, though the column suggests she tried to talk them out of the idea. In that piece, she was quoted as saying her greatest ambition was "to do her job well, and to be a good wife and homemaker." The article also touted her many skills, saying Bea Mann was "a true extrovert and handles her job with diplomacy and finesse. All of this, together with an abundance of feminine charm and innate resourcefulness and ability as a conversationalist makes her an ideal person for the position she holds."

During this period, the principal source of revenue for the Brookside Merchants Association was its membership fees. Fees consisted of basic dues plus an assessment based on each business's proximity to either of the two major parking lots in Brookside. The parking lots were the areas around the streetcar easements north and south of Sixty-third Street. They were unpaved and unkempt, but they represented precious real estate, for parking would always be at a premium in Brookside. Fees were a frequent source of contention, and the association was continually trying to adjust its calculations to reach parity, with little apparent success. Still, for the Nichols tenants, fees were included in the lease, the price of the prime location that was Brookside. But for the others, Bea Mann's "diplomacy and finesse" kept merchants appeased as best she could.

The association's records also reveal a short insight into the sensibilities of the time. Though there are few official board records during this period, there is record of a minor board action in 1968 that shows the organization's official name then as the "63rd and Brookside Business and Professional Men's Association." This name remained until at least 1974, but by the end of that decade it had reverted to the "63rd and Brookside Business Association."

Bea Mann faithfully served the organization for more than twenty years until her retirement in 1979. By then, Brookside had grown, requiring more of its association. In 1981, the merchants again selected one of their own. Virginia Kellogg had worked in Brookside with her husband, Everett, for many years, operating several different beauty salons. She knew the area well. In addition, she had some experience in event planning. Most of all, Virginia Kellogg had a dynamic personality and a flair for promotion. She was entrepreneurial before the term was common.

Brookside had its share of challenges in those days, not the least of which was a lack of marketing activity. Promotions had been strong in the late 1950s and 1960s, but by now they were few, and those had fallen into a rut. Kellogg was instrumental in the creation of Brookside's annual St. Patrick's Day parade and, most notably, its annual art fair. She was adept at promotion and found many ways to connect Brookside and its merchants to local events and to the larger Kansas City community.

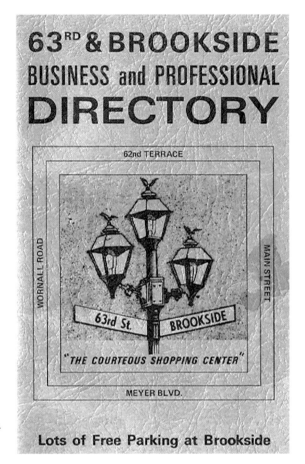

Directory of the Brookside Business Association, 1970. From the beginning until today, promotion of free parking has been considered a selling point for the Brookside Shops. *Courtesy of the author.*

In 1998, Kellogg suffered a serious injury. Realizing she could no longer devote the level of energy she had always put into Brookside, she left after seventeen years' service. That service had grown the association to such an extent that the board determined they needed greater capacity. The board contracted with the Southtown Council for professional management. The Southtown Council had already been serving business and community interests in the area south of Brush Creek, including areas adjacent to Brookside, for nearly twenty years and had recently taken on management of the Waldo Area Business Association, just south of Brookside. It was a natural alignment and a compatible arrangement that continues to the present, allowing the three associations—Brookside, Waldo and Southtown—to work cooperatively on promotions, improvements and public policy issues of common interest.

CATALOGUE: THE BROOKSIDE DOCTORS

It must have taken a good deal of confidence for young Dr. Vance Hodge to climb the stairs that first time in 1934. Only twenty-two and newly graduated, he had come to the Brookside Building looking for a place to start his dental practice. Others had told him there was only one location to consider—downtown Kansas City, of course, where all the "important" medical professionals had offices. But Dr. Hodge was looking for something else. He lived in the nearby Armour Hills neighborhood with his young and growing family and liked the idea of working close to home. From the windows of the offices he would eventually rent, he could see the streetcar turnaround on the east side of the building. A sign with his name would hang on that side of the building, and future patients getting off that streetcar would see it clearly. Somehow, he knew this little cluster of shops that served the Country Club District neighborhoods would be just the spot to start his professional life.

He wasn't alone in that feeling. By 1930, only one of the original eight medical tenants of the Brookside Building remained, but nine more would be added before the decade over. But on the south side, in Harry Jacobs's Brookside Theatre Building, another six were added during the 1930s. Brookside was an appealing location for the medical community then. It was located in the middle of the best and newest housing the city had produced. Families moving into the neighborhoods were often young and large. The location was convenient. Patients wouldn't have to spend hours traveling downtown and back. In Brookside, they could combine a dental appointment with a trip to the market or a run to the dry cleaners. And the atmosphere was friendly.

From the landlord's perspective, doctors as tenants were a boon to Brookside. They drew in customers who otherwise might never come to the area. A young girl named Virginia Hott came all the way to Brookside from her home in the Argentine neighborhood of Kansas City, Kansas, just to visit her orthodontist, Dr. Donald Closson, who had relocated there. Years later, Virginia Hott would become Virginia Kellogg, a shop owner in Brookside and ultimately the merchants' association director. "I came to Brookside for a smile," Kellogg likes to recall, "and it's given me something to smile about ever since."

But practitioners weren't the only medical presence in Brookside. From 1938 to 1945, the Jackson County Medical Milk Commission operated from the Brookside Boulevard Building, perhaps under the supervision of noted pediatrician Dr. Louis James, who also officed there. Medical Milk Commissions had been started all over the country around the turn of the century, involving physicians in certifying the hygiene standards for local milk production. And Dr. Morton Jacobs, noted psychiatrist and son of developer Harry Jacobs, operated the Brain Study Laboratory as part of his practice in his offices on Brookside Plaza.

Dr. Vance Hodge stayed in Brookside for fifty-five years. In 1976, he was joined in the practice by his son Jay, who is there today in essentially the same office, though expanded and remodeled many times. On the wall of his office hangs a proclamation by the City of Kansas City, Missouri, honoring his father when he retired in 1989. The Hodge Family Dental Practice has the distinction of being the oldest continuously operating office tenant in Brookside, as well as the oldest medical practice.

From the time of its beginnings to the present, Brookside has been the practicing home of more than 130 medical professionals of all stripes. The following is a list of those who have been in Brookside for twenty-five years or more, the years they were in Brookside, their profession and their addresses.

25 years:
- Dr. David Pyle, Psychologist, 6247 Brookside Boulevard, 1985– .

26 years:
- Dr. Louis Bono, Optometrist, 124 West Sixty-third Street, 1954–80.

28 years:
- Dr. O. Ray Penick, Dentist, 6315 Brookside Plaza, 1937–65.
- Dr. William F. Kuhn III, Physician, 6247 Brookside Boulevard, 1954–82.
- Drs. Martin M. and Deborah Isenberg, Psychologists, 6247 Brookside Boulevard, 1982– .

30 years:
- Dr. Frank A. Foyle, Dentist, 6315 Brookside Plaza, 1940–70.

35 years:
- Dr. E.C. Deffenbaugh, Dentist, 6245 Brookside Plaza, 1926–61.
- Dr. Morton Jacobs, Psychiatrist, 6314 and 6315 Brookside Plaza, 1950–83.
- Drs. Sam and Violet Smith, Chiropodists (Podiatrists), 6243 Brookside Plaza, 1954–89.

37 years:
- Dr. Joseph B. Cowherd, Physician, 6247 Brookside Boulevard, 1922–59.

- Dr. Walter C. Shull, Dentist, 6247 Brookside Boulevard, 1931–59.
- Dr. Louis M. James Jr., Orthodontist, 6247 Brookside Boulevard, 1935–72.

76 years (and counting):

- Drs. Vance (1934–1989) and Jay (1976–) Hodge, Dentists, 6247 Brookside Boulevard.

Chapter 4

THE 1940S

BROOKSIDE COMES OF AGE

As wars raged around the world, Kansas City did its part. It sent its young men to war, and at home, its women rationed, volunteered and took on jobs they never would have had in peacetime. Gone were the days of Tom Pendergast and, with them, Kansas City's somewhat sordid reputation. But through the lobbying of J.C. Nichols, who served on the Advisory Council for National Defense, wartime industry in Kansas City exploded, adding to the rising demand for workers that would have left all other businesses—including those in Brookside—strapped for help. The Fairfax plant in Kansas City, Kansas, churned out aircraft engines, and the Remington Arms plant in Independence turned out small arms ammunition. But it was no doubt the Pratt & Whitney plant at Bannister Road and Troost Avenue that had the greatest impact on Brookside.

The first twenty years in Brookside had seen steady, if modest, growth, even in the midst of the Great Depression. But the war years would bring a mixed bag of offerings to Brookside and in some ways were more difficult than the decade before. The Selective Service had an enlistment office in Brookside every year of the war, always moving around to occupy otherwise vacant space. Predictably, there was a significant drop in businesses moving into Brookside, along with an even higher number of businesses leaving and likely closing. Nineteen businesses opened up in Brookside in 1940. In both 1941 and 1942, when the war effort began in earnest, there were half that. The whole world had been turned upside down.

In Brookside it was no different. On the one hand, Brookside was now at a major crossroads of the city, thanks to the federal government, which had extended the Country Club streetcar line south to serve the new Pratt & Whitney plant. On the other hand, the pattern of commerce at the core of J.C. Nichols's shopping center model—neighborhood goods and services for the district's homemakers—was disrupted during the war years. Women joined the workforce, whether for patriotism or necessity, adding to the household income and subtracting from the time to spend it. If nothing else, the inevitable pragmatism and "back-to-basics" philosophy that such times engender no doubt cut down on household luxuries. Resources were tight, as well. So many commodities were rationed—gasoline, metals, sugar, leather, meat—that merchants were left in a bind. They easily sold out of whatever they could stock, but they couldn't find much stock to begin with. But where grocers and butchers suffered, the seamstress, the tailor and the shoe repair shop flourished. Through it all, there was one segment of the Brookside businesses that didn't seem to fade at all in the face of tough times and, in fact, thrived. Brookside was replete with clothing stores and hair salons.

FASHIONABLE BROOKSIDE

Brookside was never home to the high-fashion, big-name stores like Harzfeld's or Emery Bird Thayer. A lady or gentleman would still have to go downtown or up the road to the Country Club Plaza to find large department stores. But from the start, and particularly through the 1940s, Brookside offered everything one could want in the way of couture. Throughout the decade, Brookside averaged nearly twenty-five businesses devoted to fashion or beauty, or roughly one-third of all its shops.

To the modern sensibility, the shop offerings of that era seem quaint, often outmoded and sometimes just curious. While today only a boutique shop would sell nothing but hats, among the first Nichols tenants in the 1920s there were no fewer than three milliners. Two of them would be out of business before the 1920s were over, but one—the Shadwell Shop—continued at the northeast corner of Brookside Plaza and Sixty-third Street for thirty-three years, closing in 1970, and making it the longest-tenured business at that prominent Brookside corner. The early years, even into the 1940s, were also the time when there were still dry goods stores, the traditional term for any store selling yard goods (fabrics), textiles of any kind or products manufactured from these materials. The term "ready-to-wear" appeared often among store names, and though it, too, was a long-used term, the advent of the war had increased its popularity. "Ready-to-wear" clothes often used synthetics. Fabrics like wool, linen and silk were unobtainable because of the war effort. And while Brookside has always had one tailor or a dressmaker's shop, the 1950s would be the heyday of those professions in Brookside.

This was also the time of specialty stores, decades before the large department stores would provide one-stop shopping for a family's entire clothing needs. The B&G Hosiery Outlet Shop managed to remain fashionably relevant from 1930 to 1961. The Elizabeth Corset Salon sold—yes—corsets but also the latest articles in lingerie design, the brassiere and the girdle, which split the functions of the corset. Terry's Sportswear and Town & Country Sportswear both appeared briefly in the 1940s, selling "separates" that, during the war, emerged as a fashion trend, allowing women to mix and match and create the illusion of a larger wardrobe. And, of course, there were men's stores, though not nearly as many as would appear in the 1950s and '60s. Shapiro's Men's & Boys' Shop operated at the far west end of the Nichols shops on Sixty-third Street from 1937 to 1962.

If Brookside had a marquee name in fashion, it was surely Rothschild's. The firm of Rothschild & Son had started in nearby Leavenworth, Kansas, in the 1850s and then moved to Kansas City in 1901, where its first operation on Petticoat Lane was destroyed in a massive fire in 1909. Over the years, it continued to expand, including to the Country Club Plaza. It opened its

Circa 1937 advertisement for the Shadwell Shop at Sixty-third and Brookside Plaza, when ladies' hats were an essential wardrobe component. *Courtesy of the Brookside Business Association.*

Fashionable Rothschild's. Between 1942 and 1978, the store was the premier clothier in Brookside, located in the former Brookside Garage. *Courtesy of Wilborn & Associates.*

Brookside shop in 1942 in the space formerly occupied by the Brookside Garage and remained there until 1978, providing the finest in fashion to the ladies, gentlemen and children of the Country Club District and beyond.

Fashion might come and go in Brookside, but on the tonsorial side, Brookside barbers and beauty salons had staying power. Among the earliest tenants in Brookside was the Brookside Barber Shop. In its present location at 308 West Sixty-third Street since 1930, it has ties to Brookside's first barber, O.D. Stewart, who moved his shop to that location from the Brookside Building and then subsequently sold the operation. Fern Rush's Brookside Beauty Shop, also occupying space in the Brookside Building, operated from 1929 to 1975. Demonstrating the flourishing market for beauty in Brookside, the Ritz Beauty Shop operated right next to the Brookside Beauty Shop for almost the same duration, from 1930 to 1982. The popular Brookside Theatre Shop was opened for forty-two years and might have lasted longer had it not been destroyed in the 1978 Brookside Theatre Building fire.

The 1950s would continue as a good era for the fashion business in Brookside. When Harry Jacobs opened his new flatiron building on the west side of Brookside Plaza in 1950, the Jack Norman Shop for Men was the first tenant in the prominent glass surround of the building's anchor space. The locally popular shops the Village Set for women and Mister Guy for men both had a Brookside presence in the 1960s and early '70s. But few of the stores that had been there in the 1950s were still there by the '60s, and by then, fashion no longer dominated the Brookside Shops in the same way. The large department stores in suburban malls offered a variety (and sometimes a price) that proved stiff competition for the smaller Brookside shops. For the past thirty years, only about 10 percent of Brookside Shops have catered to fashion and beauty.

BROOKSIDE'S ROADS AND RAILS

J.C. Nichols knew the "motorcar" was the vehicle taking America to the future. Building quality roads in the Country Club District was a priority. He was involved in the City Beautiful movement and worked with famed planner and landscape architect George Kessler on both his own residential projects and larger civic endeavors. Brookside was designed to be auto-friendly. As early as 1920, Nichols published a map of the "Scenic Route Through the Country Club District," with the printed suggestion, "Put this in the pocket of your automobile for use the next time you are pleasure driving."

But first, there was the streetcar. The streetcar line had served Nichols well in his first development, Bismark Place. He used it to extend the attractiveness of the Country Club District to Sixty-third Street and beyond, as well as along Ward Parkway for a time. In the years leading up to the Brookside groundbreaking, the Metropolitan Street Railway Company that operated the city's streetcars then reported what would be an all-time record ridership of more than 135 million riders annually. The system would never see numbers like that again. It wouldn't be until 1945 that ridership would near that level, but by that time, ridership counts included both streetcars and buses.

But it is this strange combination of streetcar riders, automobile drivers and bus passengers that made this a golden time for transportation at the Brookside Shops, even as the streetcar system throughout the rest of the city was struggling. A trip from Brookside to downtown on the Country Club Line was a great adventure. A person could travel from the tranquility

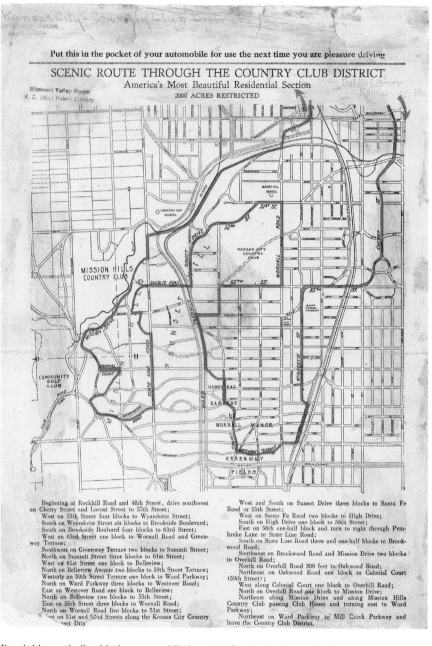

Brookside was built with the automobile in mind. In this 1920 map, Nichols promotes scenic drives through the Country Club District. *Courtesy of the Missouri Valley Special Collections, Kansas City Public Library, Kansas City, MO.*

of tree-lined streets to the exotic views of the Plaza, then north on Main buzzing along with the traffic as the car slipped past apartment buildings and warehouses and then finally to the glittering canyons of downtown, filled with the allure of the department store windows. Or maybe the ride was more prosaic. A rider might have grabbed a bus to get to Brookside and then transferred to the streetcar for the ride to Pratt & Whitney for that new, much-needed wartime job. The trip would have shot south along Wornall Road until it reached the community of Waldo, then southeast toward Dodson and, finally, the new track the federal government built to reach the P&W plant. Regardless of the trip, the gateway to all these adventures and more was the transit stop on the west side of Brookside Plaza, just north of Sixty-third Street.

Though the streetcars in Kansas City had never been profitable, they were always highly popular. Time and again, as ridership declined and routes were threatened, the community came out in support of the line. There were no

A dapper gentleman meets the Country Club Line (#56) streetcar as it pulls into the Brookside Station, circa 1950. When the city finally discontinued streetcar service, this was the last line to run. *Courtesy of Wilborn & Associates.*

stauncher supporters than those in the Brookside area, no doubt one of the reasons the Country Club Line was the last line to run. In 1947, motorbuses outnumbered streetcars for the first time, and the decline continued from there. Ten years later, with a ridership of only forty-six million annually, the Country Club Line made its last run.

Just having the streetcar nearby was stimulation for the imagination of Brookside youth. In the early 1940s, a young Howard Gadberry lived just north of Brookside in one of the houses adjacent to the streetcar line. As an adult, Gadberry would become an accomplished chemist for Midwest Research Institute just up the road, but back then, he was only a budding scientist. In the wee hours before a summer's dawn, well in advance of the streetcar's first run of the morning, young Howard and a friend slipped out of their homes and walked a long stretch of the rail. For about a dozen blocks, in intervals of twenty feet or so, they carefully placed a penny-sized mound of a small compound they had mixed in their home laboratory. Then they hid, waiting eagerly for the streetcar to come. It rolled over the tracks until it reached the powder mounds. *Bang! Bang! Bang!* The driver stopped the car. He looked out and saw the piles ahead on the track. He grabbed a broom and started sweeping the rails, but soon he looked up again. As far as he could see in the dim morning light, there were the little mounds of powder. Defeated, he threw his broom back on the car and went on, much to the delight of the boys, who laughed so hard they lost count of the explosions.

The rails the boys had employed to such amusement remained intact long after the Country Club Line was gone. To the neighborhood, they were a nostalgic reminder of days gone by. To others, they marked a critical easement, a valuable piece of property with potential for many purposes. That easement would one day prove to be a chink in the protective armor Nichols had so carefully built for the district.

When Nichols first started on the Country Club District, he saw the nearby rail line as both an opportunity and a threat. Built in the 1880s as a private railway, the tracks hauled freight the eight miles between Westport and the small community of Dodson. It earned the name the "Dodson dummy line" because as a freight train (sometimes with a couple of open passenger cars attached) running through residential areas, its dirty steam engine was outwardly clad to resemble the horse-drawn cars. This was to appease homeowners. The opportunity was the fact that there was an existing rail line that already took passengers, however irregularly. The threat was that it was a freight line, which Nichols feared would attract industry into an area he was working hard to transform into upscale neighborhoods. Nichols bought the line for $15,000 and then turned it over to the Metropolitan Street Railway Company, which operated the city's public streetcar system. In addition, Nichols offered "the Met" a $50,000 bonus on the completion of two conditions: that the line be electrified and that it never service freight. The Met conformed to the electrification requirements but refused the freight provision and never got the bonus.

As a result, some share of the easement of the rail remained in private hands, even though over time, the streetcar system eventually transferred to the Kansas City Public Service Company and then to the hands of the Kansas City Area Transportation Authority. Over the years, there were repeated attempts through litigation and condemnation to reclaim the full right-of-way for a variety of purposes, including at one point a freeway. Those plans never came to fruition, but in the 1990s, the easement was converted to a bike and pedestrian trail dubbed the "Harry Wiggins Trolley Track Trail," named for the longtime state senator who helped secure funding for the trail. While alliterative, the name is historically misleading. The Country Club Line was a streetcar line, never a trolley bus line.

CATALOGUE: ARCHITECTURAL STYLES AND INFLUENCES

By the 1940s, all of Brookside's major architectural styles and influences were in place, and only a few minor stylistic changes have occurred since then. Architecture played a central role in Brookside's development. The faux English Tudor style of the original Nichols shops came from a sketch by landscape architect John Nolen given to J.C. Nichols, responding to Nichols's intent to make sure the Brookside Shops reflected the surrounding neighborhood architecture. Yet that residential architecture itself is highly varied, so the choice of English Tudor is somewhat arbitrary. It is worth noting that the three other Nichols commercial properties contemporary to Brookside had very different styles. The Colonial Shops were, well, Colonial, but only by virtue of the columnar supports for the low overhang above the façade. The façades of the Crestwood Shops are Early Classical revival, while the Country Club Plaza is famous for its Spanish architecture with Moorish influences.

The architecture of the Country Club District homes is even more diverse. Within those acres of houses there are worthy examples of every residential style of the first half of the twentieth century. From Beaux-Arts to Italian

Bill Drummond (Drummond Cleaners) built this deco-façade building at 6328 Brookside Plaza to relocate his dry cleaners in 1938. The black-and-white glass tile and neon details are now gone. *Courtesy of the Brookside Business Association.*

Another Brookside architectural landmark, Harry Jacobs's Brookside Plaza Building, circa 1953. Its Art Moderne styling fits well with its flatiron design. *Courtesy of Wilborn & Associates.*

Renaissance, from Colonial Revival to Craftsman, from French Eclectic to, yes, English Tudor, all are present in abundance. It is just that diversity of style that has helped to maintain the Country Club District's appeal and stability. In the subtle shifts through middle-, upper-middle- and upper-income housing that move roughly east to west within the district, there are no sharp edges, no stark changes in style that signal a sudden shift in income or status. Only the size of the houses and lots make those distinctions, and even here the changes are gradual.

But among the commercial styles of the Brookside Shops there are only a few distinct types. The following might serve as a general guide for a walking tour of Brookside's architectural highlights.

- English Tudor—The English Tudor styling of the original Nichols properties on the north side of Sixty-third Street is characterized by exposed half timbers across the stucco cladding of the upper floors or gables, the brick or stone cladding of the street level façades, stone casements and entryways (most apparent on the Station Building) and details such as small paned windows leaded on the diagonal and crenellated roof and gable ridges. This style remains consistent through the old Nichols properties, with the exception of 12 West Sixty-third Street, which has a more rustic, wood-clad English country style.
- Early Classical Revival—Burned down in 1978, the old Brookside Theatre Building was a modern interpretation of the Early Classical Revival style popular in the late eighteenth to mid-nineteenth centuries. It boasted a dominant gable front, and its sharp, straight lines were accentuated by white moldings. Other classic elements of the building included arched windows, a roofline balustrade and a small circular window above the somewhat truncated front portico. The large electrified sign on the roof and the Art Deco style of the movie theatre's marquee were more in keeping with the architectural styles contemporary to the building's construction.
- Art Deco—While much of the detail of Brookside's Art Deco buildings is now hidden by modern façades, some elements are still visible. The buildings that can legitimately claim that heritage include 113–121 West Sixty-third Street, 6307 Brookside Plaza and 6322–6330 Brookside Plaza. While none of these is an example of Art Deco at its most dramatic, each has or had elements of the horizontal, geometric motifs that characterize the style. A particular loss is the sharp jewel-cut display windows surrounded by black glass that were featured at

117 and 121 West Sixty-third Street. These were also present at 6330 Brookside Plaza, which had a striking black-and-white glass tile and neon façade. The best current examples of that deco style are much different. Small multicolored terra cotta reliefs are still visible above the awnings at 6320 and 6322 Brookside Plaza, as are the brilliant terrazzo sunbursts at the threshold of each of those two addresses.

- Art Moderne—The name for the later period of Art Deco design, Art Moderne is mostly characterized by a sleeker, horizontal line than Art Deco and was almost always used in commercial, rather than residential, settings. Brookside is fortunate to have an excellent example of the period. The Brookside Plaza Building, which includes addresses from 6304 to 6314 Brookside Plaza, has the classic traits—smooth, monochromatic surfaces, a flat roof, horizontal lines accentuated by polished metalwork and a curved window. The building's flatiron (triangular) shape fits well with the design, but the flatiron style actually dates originally to the late 1890s and is designed to take advantage of irregularly shaped lots.

Chapter 5

THE 1950S

BOOMER DAYS IN BROOKSIDE

Looking back, J.C. Nichols's vision for the Country Club District seems best suited to an idealized vision of America in the 1950s. Where just a generation before there had been open fields and gravel roads, now there were tree-lined streets through tidy neighborhoods. The neighborhoods themselves brimmed with young families who filled the district's parks, schools and, most particularly for Brookside, its shops. The Country Club District had spread to the four corners Nichols had originally envisioned, as the Prairie Village subdivision finally came on line. It is sadly ironic, then, that Nichols never lived to see his Country Club District during this era. He died in February 1950, after a brief illness. His role as president of the Nichols Company was assumed by his son Miller, so the transition was seamless. But the 1950s would be the period where the strength of J.C. Nichols's legacy would first be tested.

For the most part, the 1950s were good to the Brookside Shops, and they in turn were good to the community. The period from 1950 to 1959 saw the greatest increase in new businesses in Brookside to date. During those ten years, more than 150 different stores or offices would open in Brookside, owing largely to the last big increase in development that Brookside would ever see. Harry Jacobs built his final building at 6314 Brookside Plaza, an impressive flatiron building in the streamlined look of the era. The 1950s also saw the greatest number of business carryovers from one decade to the next. Brookside was stable, and its businesses were now stalwarts of the community, already passing from one generation to the next.

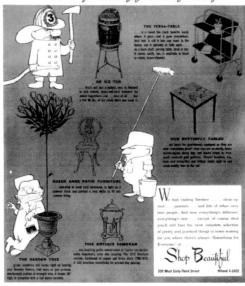

Above: Aerial view of Brookside, circa 1950, looking northeast. The Brookside Theatre sign clashed with Nichols's original design but served as a ready landmark for the area. *Courtesy of the Brookside Business Association*.

Left: Society magazine *The Independent* has long been a major advertising vehicle for Brookside Shops. In 1959, Shop Beautiful artfully made a promotional event out of a recent fire. *Courtesy of* The Independent.

ONE FAMILY'S ENTERPRISE: THE COUNTRY CLUB SHOE STORE

Many of Brookside's longest lasting and most popular businesses have been family affairs. Among others, the Dime Store, Drummond Cleaners, Shop Beautiful and Crick Camera all owe their success in part to the tradition of the family business in Brookside. None better exemplifies this tradition than the Country Club Shoe Store.

Jacob Hyman left Poland in 1908, arriving in Kansas City to open a shoe repair shop at Thirty-first Street and Holmes Road, near the center of Kansas City's Jewish community. His business grew, and in 1922 he moved to the small commercial center at Fifty-ninth Street and Brookside Boulevard. It was at this location that he began to sell shoes, specifically children's shoes. He soon built a good following, which brought him to the attention of the Nichols Company. In 1934, they enticed him to relocate to 122 West Sixty-third Street. It was newly finished space—Hyman would be the first tenant—and in a prime location at the center of the shops.

Jake Hyman had married late in life and had no children. He had two brothers in Kansas City, but they had left behind a sister. After the invasion of Poland in 1939, he lost track of her family. Only after the war would he learn that his sister and her son, Leon, had spent the war in a labor camp. Leon's father had not survived. The Hyman brothers began preparations for bringing them to America.

Young Leon arrived first, in June 1949. Leon was immediately taken into his uncle Jacob's house as a son. His aunt insisted they enroll Leon in Paseo High School right away, even though he was already nineteen and the school year was all but over. She reasoned the best thing they could do for Leon was to see that he fit in. He knew some English, but that would need to be improved, of course. And he would need to make friends and learn about America. It was at her suggestion that he changed his German surname to its English translation. He became Leon Goodhart.

Leon would continue with school for a while. In the fall, he enrolled in Southwest High School, and later he attended a bit of college. All the while, he worked part time for his uncle. He was thrilled with the opportunity. America was "the land I had dreamed about," he said, and working side by side with his uncle at the shoe store seemed a good life. He recognized that his uncle, already a successful businessman for forty years, could teach him more than any college. Leon also saw the high regard others had for

From left: Leon Goodhart of the Country Club Shoe Store with other newly elected Brookside Merchants Association officers Charles McGowan (University Bank), Ernest Arfsten (Arfsten's Dime Store) and Dennis Doyle (Surface Paints), 1971. *Courtesy of the Brookside Business Association.*

his uncle—both merchants and customers, many of whom were among the Country Club District's most elite residents.

Leon was a natural at the business. He was bright and hardworking and had a manner the customers liked. He had a strong business ethic taken both from his uncle and his father, who ran a trucking business back in Poland, always on the basis of a handshake between gentlemen. Leon, too, was always as good as his word. He was well liked among the merchants and quickly became involved in the mercantile life of Brookside.

At the store, Leon learned a great deal from his uncle, but he tried to make his own mark on the store, too, though often he came up against his uncle's more traditional views. On small matters, as time went by he would make changes according to his "new" ideas on his uncle's day off. Many times, when Jacob would return, he would let Leon have his way, once he could see the logic of the idea. But other times, Jacob Hyman would put his foot down. That was what happened when it came to the Pedoscopes, the X-ray machines so popular in shoe stores in the 1940s and 1950s. They were marketed as a means of diagnosing children's feet. The child would slip his feet into a slot at the bottom of the cabinet, just over the X-ray tube. On top, there were three viewers that allowed the salesman, the child and his mother to look at the image of the skeletal feet. Jacob Hyman wanted no part of the Pedoscopes, though Leon repeatedly argued that they were a proven draw for customers. Hyman deplored gimmicks, so the Country Club Shoe Store never had one. As early as 1950, the radiation hazards posed by the machines were recognized, although it took as much as twenty years more for them to be banned.

But Jacob Hyman had his own visions for the store. He already owned a small retail building with two storefronts, at 6320–6322 Brookside Plaza. He had built it in the late 1930s, shortly after Harry Jacobs completed the Brookside Theatre Building across the street. With Leon now at the store, Hyman had the opportunity to buy the adjacent property. He built another retail space at 6318 Brookside Plaza, intending to eventually move the shoe store. But through a miscommunication with his friend, a real estate broker who handled leases for his property next door, a lease was signed with another merchant. Hyman never moved the shoe store there. After a while, he began to see the wisdom of leasing the space for the store and keeping the other property as a second source of income. Over the years, those two buildings were home to such Brookside notables as Crick Camera, Le Chateaubriand, Dos Hombres and the first Bagel & Bagel.

Leon was in Kansas City only two years before he was drafted. He served with the medical corps in Korea even before he became a citizen. Shortly after he returned, he married and started his own family. He came back to stay with his uncle Jake at the shoe store until Hyman retired in 1958. With no other heirs, Hyman sold the business and property to his nephew. By now, Goodhart had become the venerable merchant of Brookside his uncle had been before him, and the Country Club Shoe Store was starting on its third generation of customers.

As successful as the Country Club Shoe Store had been under Jacob Hyman, it was the postwar baby boomer years that put the business indelibly on the Brookside map. A seemingly endless stream of mothers and children came through the doors, shopping for back-to-school shoes, Christmas shoes, Easter shoes, gym shoes and ballet shoes. A trip to the Country Club Shoe Store marked the passing of the seasons and the special times in a child's life. Even then, the next generation was getting its first taste of the business. Leon's oldest son, Doug, spent Friday afternoons passing out toys to the children who came to the shop. He learned other lessons from his father, too, for he kept his earnings in a savings account in a Brookside bank.

Now that the Country Club Shoe Store was his, Goodhart made some changes. He saw several opportunities. One was in providing orthopedic shoes for children, a market the store covered so well that not only was it the store to which orthopedists most commonly referred their patients, but Leon was also frequently invited to work with many of the orthopedic practices in town, instructing new doctors on the corrective benefits of children's footwear. Similarly, when his customers started asking for ballet shoes, he bought for that market, too. And he expanded his locations. In the 1940s, Jacob Hyman had opened a second store on the Country Club Plaza, but the wartime rationing of leather had made it hard for him to stock one store, let alone two, and so he closed it and kept his focus on Brookside. In the 1960s, Goodhart opened a second store again, this time in the newly opened Corinth Shopping Center at Eighty-third Street and Mission Road in

When the Country Club Shoe Store remodeled in 1964, it warranted a feature article in the *Wednesday Magazine. Courtesy of Sun Publications.*

Kansas, a later period Nichols Company center. Though that store operated for twenty-eight years, eventually it exclusively catered to the dancewear customers he had first cultivated in Brookside. In his final years at the store, Goodhart recognized the times were changing for the shoe business. Many of his longtime competitors had closed. The children's market wasn't enough to keep in business. He started again to sell adult shoes, being the first to introduce quality brand names like New Balance to the Kansas City market. But one thing never changed. Goodhart always maintained high standards of service and brought to his customers in Brookside the very finest quality product available.

When Leon Goodhart finally retired in 1995, he turned the business over to his son Doug, the same son who had worked there as a child passing out toys. Just one year short of its seventieth year in Brookside, Doug Goodhart made the difficult decision to relocate the store farther south to accommodate both his own family's needs and to be closer to the store's market. But Leon Goodhart stayed in Brookside as a property owner. About the time he retired, he purchased the building at 6314 Brookside Plaza from Jacobs Properties, which gave him the lion's share of the property on the west side of Brookside Plaza. But for Goodhart, the property—like the shoe store—has always been more than an investment. And even though the Country Club Shoe Store is no longer in Brookside, the legacy of family that started with Jacob Hyman—a legacy of service, integrity and pride of place—continues to influence the character of the Brookside Shops.

THE DWELLERS UPSTAIRS

With the completion of Harry Jacobs's final building on the west side of Brookside Plaza in 1950, Brookside had in excess of fifty office spaces on the floors above the various shops, just slightly fewer than half of the total number of Brookside tenants. Yet with the exception of the doctors, dentists and occasional hairstylist, few of these businesses drew much walk-in traffic. They were largely invisible to the casual Brookside shopper, yet their influence was significant. Many of the office dwellers were residents of the district, and the jobs they held represented among the highest wages to be earned in Brookside. They also show the diversity of business in Brookside, with a surprising array of quirky and curious lines.

It was in the 1950s that these businesses—often referred to collectively as "manufacturers' agents"—proliferated in Brookside. Sales representatives were a growing category of worker. The war had created both technology and demand for new products of all sorts. Sales offices were small operations that could serve a large geography from almost any location. Whereas the modern model is often to work out of the home, this was an era when having an outside office was still required to seem legitimate. For a resident of nearby neighborhoods, Brookside offered a convenient, reasonably priced space at the crossroads of transportation. And, of course, these tenants provided the retail shops with a regular customer base. An office worker could drop off dry cleaning on the way to work, squeeze in a dental appointment during the day, enjoy a reasonably priced lunch and do some grocery shopping on the way home, all within the confines of the Brookside Shops.

Though the 1950s were the heyday of these businesses, they were present from the beginning, though scant. In 1929, the Radio Cinema Company marketed a new technology for the simultaneous broadcasting of pictures and sound—the first iteration of television broadcasting. The company was only in Brookside for a year. Between 1930 and 1950, three different fuel distributors worked out of Brookside. After World War II, the presence of the manufacturers' agent in Brookside grew deep and wide. They sold lumber, hospital supplies, diesel engines and vacuum cleaners. They represented automotive suppliers, underground storage facilities, electronics manufacturers, industrial equipment and home cleaning products. Many, no doubt, saw Brookside as a central location for the products and services they sold for the home and family.

Others, particularly in those first postwar years, may have located there because they sold equipment to the Pratt & Whitney plant, connected to Brookside by the streetcar line. One such vendor, and perhaps one of Brookside's most unique tenants, was the Nukem Products Corporation, which came to Brookside in 1952 selling "Nukemite." The November 1949 issue of *Modern Mechanix* provided directions for bronzing baby shoes. According to the instructions, the trickiest part of the process was the construction of the plating tank. The article's author wholeheartedly endorsed the use of Nukemite because it was impervious to chemicals, dried quickly and created a rubberlike lining. However, Nukemite had another use more fitting its name. In 1951, the American Institute of Architects and the Atomic Energy Commission published the proceedings of its conference on laboratory design for handling radioactive materials. In that publication, Nukemite is listed as one of the acceptable coatings for walls and surfaces for atomic laboratories, because in the event of contamination, it could be peeled from the walls. It seems more likely that the Nukem Corporation was located in Brookside to take advantage of a major customer, Pratt & Whitney, than to preserve the shoes of Country Club District babies.

Over the years, more than seventy manufacturing agent businesses have called Brookside home, mostly during the 1950s and 1960s. From then on, these special tenants were rarer and never lasted in Brookside more than a few years. But while they reigned, the sales representatives that called Brookside home represented a significant part of the area's economy.

CATALOGUE: CHILDHOOD HAUNTS

To be a child in the neighborhoods around the Brookside Shops after 1950 would be akin to living around the corner from paradise. On a Saturday afternoon, kids could ride their bikes into Brookside and fill their entire day with childhood adventures. There was the Brookside Theatre, of course, which not only ran popular movies but also had special promotions for prizes and free tickets. If the theatre's candy and popcorn weren't enough, a kid

There's always been something to draw children to Brookside, like this yo-yo competition at House of Toys (Brookside Toy & Gift) in 1963. *Courtesy of Sun Publications.*

might find himself in line at the Velvet Freeze on Sixty-third Street, waiting for that chocolate cone, or spending the last of his pennies on something from Smith's Candies right next door to the theatre, or maybe just ogling the baked goodies displayed so beautifully in the window of the Cake Box across the street. For older kids with greater freedom and more money in their pockets, the afternoon could be pleasantly passed with friends at the soda fountain at the Parkview Drug Store at Brookside Plaza and Sixty-third Street, or at Katz's Drugs at Sixty-third Street and Brookside Boulevard, or maybe going through the record bins at the Brookside Record Shop. Below is a listing of just some of the Brookside shops that have held such fascination for the youngsters of Brookside.

- Old Colony Book Shop—6237, and later 6231, Brookside Plaza, 1926–68.
- Betty Jane Ice Cream Shop—126 West Sixty-third Street, 1930–49.
- Mrs. Stover's Bungalow Candies—6306 Brookside Plaza, 1935–42.
- Brookside Theatre—6325 Brookside Plaza, 1937–78.
- Modern Book Shop—6323 Brookside Plaza, 1937–78. *The Modern Book Shop was the place many area children went to get their textbooks and school supplies. On some days before the start of the school year, the line to get in would wind around the corner.*
- Amy Winning, Piano Teacher—6315 Brookside Plaza, 1939–68. *Though one of the original tenants of the Brookside Theatre Building, Ms. Winning finished her tenure in Brookside in a converted residence on Sixty-second Terrace, near the site of the current Cosentino's Market.*
- Brookside Record Shop—6330 Brookside Plaza, 1946–52.
- Brookside Toy & Science—330 West Sixty-third Street, and earlier 6237 Brookside Boulevard, 1947– . *The shop has changed ownership over the years and, with it, the name. For its first few years, the shop was called Brookside Game & Gift, but it changed in 1953 to Brookside Toy & Gift. When it moved to Sixty-third Street, the name changed again to Brookside Toy & Hobbies, and then again in the mid-1980s to Brookside Toy & Science.*
- Velvet Freeze Ice Cream—105 West Sixty-third Street, 1951–79.
- Baskin-Robbins Ice Cream—6309 Brookside Plaza and 336 West Sixty-third Street, 1964– . *Originally in the Brookside Theatre Building, it moved to its present location in 1978 following the fire.*
- Foo's Fabulous Frozen Custard—6235 Brookside Plaza, 1989– .
- Reading Reptile—326 West Sixty-third Street: 2003– .

Chapter 6

THE 1960S

"The Courteous Shopping Center"

The great political and social upheavals that would come to be associated with the 1960s were still percolating as the decade began. The explosive, landmark year of 1968 would change almost everything in America, but earlier the world—and Kansas City along with it—was growing so fast the landscape sometimes changed in weeks and with it the sense of value. For the Brookside Shops, the change meant competition.

Consider the influences as those in Brookside might have at the time. The actual size of the metropolitan area was exploding and would double by decade's end. Many of the city's notable structures built in the boom of the 1880s were being iron-balled for newer buildings—or parking lots. The federal government was funding urban renewal projects, including much of the interstate system that belts Kansas City today. These projects were bulldozing buildings in the old centers and connecting people to new centers miles away. Retail competition was everywhere. The late 1950s through the '60s saw the construction of the Blue Ridge Mall, the Ward Parkway Shopping Center and Crown Center. Even the Nichols Company was building more retail centers like Prairie Village and Corinth.

The merchants of Brookside, now acting fully as their own association (though still with much support from the Nichols Company), made two important moves during this period. The first was to hire their first secretary to help manage the details of the association. The second was to promote Brookside in every way they could imagine. As it turned out, both their new employee and their imaginations were highly productive.

It might have been because of those changing times that the Brookside merchants chose "Brookside—the Courteous Shopping Center" as the new slogan in 1960. The Brookside Shops still had a market advantage in a world of increasingly high-paced, low-service retail. Where other shopping centers promoted the latest and greatest, Brookside would focus on traditions, families and community. These values were at the core of a promotional idea that proved successful and popular, though it had a rocky start.

Students from Southwest High School were invited to submit drawings for murals to be painted in shop windows, and a panel of judges composed of merchants would judge and award prizes. The first contest was tied to the district's annual Mother's Day promotion. Despite the fact that the association's secretary, Bea Miller, visited all the shops to encourage participation, it was an embarrassment to the association's board when only a small percentage participated. Association President Stanford Saper sent

Winners of the first annual Easter window display contest were three students from Southwest High School. *From left*: Adrienne Gotlieb, Carla Schultz and Sue McClelland congratulated by Charles McGowan of University Bank. *Courtesy of the Brookside Business Association.*

a letter to the members he addressed as "the Sleepy 63rd and Brookside Association," admonishing them that "unless this area awakens and the merchants do everything in their power to cooperate with each other, the shopping areas around us will gradually smother us and our volume will diminish rapidly."

It may have been this letter, or perhaps the lure of a fancier promotion, that had nearly all the merchants participating just a month later. The Brookside Theatre was to premiere the movie *Can-Can*, starring Frank Sinatra and Shirley MacLaine. This time, the promotion would go beyond mere window displays. Parisian-style café tables with checkered tablecloths sat in front of the stores. Merchants were encouraged to create their own promotions offering anything that could be remotely connected to the theme. Advertising in the *Wednesday Magazine* featured the slogan, "Nobody Can Can, like the Brookside Merchants Can." The Kansas City Ballet sponsored the event as a benefit. A parade of French marque automobiles drove dignitaries to the theatre.

Brookside promotions were often tied to charitable events, as with this white elephant sale for Children's Mercy Hospital, held in the middle of Brookside Plaza, 1961. *Courtesy of the Brookside Business Association.*

The painting of the windows continued as a promotional event for several years, and Southwest High School students continued to compete for prizes donated by the merchants. Eventually, the window paintings became most closely associated with the Easter holiday sales. Until its demise in the late 1970s, the Brookside Theatre would continue as Brookside's best advertising venue, and time and again promotional events would be tied to movie premieres.

Many other promotions were tried during this period, rarely lasting more than a few years. The merchants tried "Royal Days," in conjunction with the annual American Royal, though the promotion itself seems to have little to do with Kansas City's cowtown heritage. The police department brought their trained dogs, and a pony ring was set up to give free rides to children. Parents could register their children for a grand prize—the winner's choice of a pony or a bicycle. The winner chose the bike. There was also "Girl Scout Day," "Family Night" (Thursdays), a contest to finish the sentence in twenty-five words or less, "I Like to Shop at Brookside Because..." and the first gift certificates. Promotions continue through to the present, but eventually Brookside would become known more for major events like the Art Annual than for the promotional gimmickry of the 1960s.

THE ROAD TO NOWHERE: THE COUNTRY CLUB FREEWAY

The urban renewal work in Kansas City at this time was part of a national movement born largely of the contemporaneous policy thinking that the only cure for the increasing blight of America's inner cities was to lay waste to the decay using public funds to build "efficient" highways that would stimulate new development outside the urban core. Such practices were already being called into question by 1960. These projects were tearing apart the poorest neighborhoods, and as those neighborhoods were often minority communities, urban renewal added to the growing awareness of racial imbalance in the country. But in 1960, these groups did not yet have the public voice they would gain in a few years. Groups that did have voice, like the well-off residents of the Country Club District, with their neighborhoods planned for permanence by J.C. Nichols himself, would surely have felt insulated from the threat of urban renewal. Yet they were wrong.

As early as 1958, there were discussions at city hall about the possibility of a freeway through the Country Club District. Traffic was a major problem in the city. Those who lived in the suburbs wanted speedy access to downtown and other points in the metro. There were interstate highway projects in the works. The time seemed right to many, including the Nichols Company. After J.C.'s death in 1950, the company had continued an impressive pace of development. While still technically connected to the original Country Club District at many points, much of its current development was in what seemed in 1960 a fair distance, on the southern fringes of the metropolitan area. The Nichols Company saw the Country Club Freeway as a boon to that development.

In late 1959, the city began to work on condemning the streetcar right-of-way as the basis for the freeway. They intended to take it all, from Eighty-fifth Street and Prospect Avenue all the way north to Westport. Advertised in modest notices in the local paper, neighborhood meetings were held where City Councilman Charles Shafer Jr. met with residents to explain the city's plan and answer questions. The whole proceeding started out quietly and, for eighteen months, seemed to have made only a modest impression on the community.

Those whose houses directly abutted the streetcar line did pay attention, however. When the matter finally came before the Jackson County Circuit Court in June 1961, those homeowners were represented at the hearing by a phalanx of some fifty lawyers, requesting damages on behalf of their clients. Collectively, it was their contention that the condemnation of the rail line represented a loss in the value of their homes, and they should be compensated. Ultimately, this argument did not hold, but the litigation had raised the attention of the entire community.

The city's point man was associate City Counselor Herbert Hoffman. He had been in charge of the condemnation action and so became the city's de facto advocate for the freeway. He was diligent but hampered in his efforts toward progress. There were questions about ownership of the actual line that would plague the easement for years to come. The original condemnation ordinance was determined too weak to prevail in court, forcing him back to city council for revision, which ultimately caused delays that allowed time for opposition to coalesce. That opposition was in full force by September 1961. The community meetings had far outgrown the small churches where they started. In the auditorium of Southwest High School, a panel came to discuss the project. For the first time, the Missouri Highway Department's man described what the proposed freeway would be like. The plan called for a six-lane, high-speed (forty-five-mile-per-hour), non-access highway, meaning limited places for entrance and exit. It would connect with both the northern and southern tracks of the new interstate highway loop around the city. In the bounds of the Country Club District and south, most of the road surface would be below grade, twenty feet or more, with only occasional bridges to allow cars and people to cross from one side to the other. When the freeway continued north, it would come within a block of the Plaza and then rise above grade courtesy of a concrete viaduct and somehow meander northeast to connect with the interstate there. Worst of all, it would require two hundred feet of right-of-way on either side of these proposed six lanes, meaning it would cut a swath through the Country Club District that could easily obliterate all structures between Oak Street to the east and halfway between Wornall Road and Ward Parkway to the west. The Brookside Shops were in jeopardy, and along with them Brookside Boulevard, the Waldo area and countless homes and other businesses.

The description surely horrified those in attendance and those who read of the plans in the local paper. Almost immediately, varying proposals began to be offered by those in city hall, including one councilman's suggestion to

These cover photos from the October 11, 1961 *Wednesday Magazine* impressed the Brookside area residents with the consequences of the proposed Country Club Freeway. *Courtesy of Sun Publications.*

completely bury the freeway through the area. Some called to update the streetcar line to accommodate one of the new modes of mass transit being explored in other cities, such as a monorail. But even in the Brookside area, the freeway had its supporters who thought it represented opportunity. Freeway supporters expressed faith that the city, state and local governments would make certain any plan would not disrupt the neighborhood. Opponents were more cynical. The topic spawned grass-roots community organizing and the formation of at least a couple of so-called "betterment" associations.

For the next year, there was much discussion but no resolution. Opponents and supporters alike showed up in increasing numbers at court hearings and city council meetings. Everyone seemed to be waiting for a decision on the final plan or the condemnation proceedings to conclude. Then, in 1963, it was time to elect a new city council and a new mayor. No candidate wanted controversy, and the freeway was certainly that. There was growing awareness that there were far more people now opposed than in favor. In July 1965, the Jackson County Circuit Court dismissed the city's condemnation suit, forever closing its option on construction of the Country Club Freeway. In the end, the public outcries and political will of the Country Club residents didn't stop it—it was simply a question of law. The court dismissed the case on the grounds that, as property already owned by a public entity (the Public Service Transit Company), the city couldn't condemn the line. It would be another thirty years before the right-of-way question was resolved.

As to the freeway, earlier that spring, the Missouri State Highway Commission, no doubt frustrated by the city's inability to move forward on the project, revised its recommendation. According to the *Wednesday Magazine*, the commission proposed "a route farther east…for the south-town freeway, partly because it would not cost as much money as the Country Club Streetcar Route." Forty years later, that eastern road was completed, congruent with Missouri 71 Highway, and named Bruce R. Watkins Drive.

Rags, Brookside's Favorite Resident

He was just a mongrel from the pound, a scruffy mix of Airedale and sheepdog. He cost his owner, Hy Davidson, one whole dollar to take home to the family house at Sixty-third Street and Ward Parkway. But the dog's affable, tail-wagging ways earned Rags a special place in the Brookside community. He was allowed to accompany the Davidson children to school—Border Star and Southwest High School. And during part of his

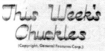

Magazine

| VOLUME 25 | Reg. U. S. Pat. Off. | KANSAS CITY, MISSOURI, MARCH 28, 1962 | Silver Jubilee — |

This Week's Chuckles
(Copyright, General Features Corp.)

The biggest difference between men and boys is the cost of their toys.

It may be face powder that gets a man, but it's baking powder that keeps him.

A working girl is one who quit her job to get married.

If you are dissatisfied with the way things are done in Washington, just remember — you don't have to like everything about the Government, but you certainly have to hand it to the Internal Revenue Service.

It's easy to tell those who have never had much experience in committee work — they always get to the meetings on time.

Scientists say man is a modified plant. This may account for all the blooming idiots along the highway!

Mankind might take a lesson from the snowflake: No two are like and yet look how beautifully they work together on major accomplishments, such as tying up traffic.

RAGS LIVES HERE

Here . . . . . ? Well, not exactly, he lives just about any place he is welcome. If you should inquire, you'll find it's almost any place in the general vicinity of 63rd and Brookside. Now, wait a minute, if you are thinking he is a stray dog, read on . . . . for that is definitely not the case. He belongs to the H. Davidson family, but Rags needs a broader scope for his affection than just one family. You see, he's a real cosmopolitan and must make his daily rounds to dispense affection and see that all his friends are in good shape. No foolish barking, fawning and begging for him, no sir! Rags has a genuine dignity and expects to be treated similarly.

Rags, the unofficial mascot of Brookside in the late 1950s and early 1960s. *Courtesy of Sun Publications.*

day—every day—Rags would make the rounds of Brookside. Better known than some of the merchants, Rags was a regular at many spots in Brookside, including the fire station, Hogerty's Lounge, Lu Gaines Travel Agency, the Parkview Drug Store and Malang's House of Design. He was greeted and fussed over wherever he went. Surely, this was canine heaven.

Then the Davidson family moved west, to Sixty-fourth Street and Verona Road. Rags, by then an elderly dog of ten years or so, would have none of it. He continued to come to Brookside when he could escape, despite the physical toll all the fence jumping and long walks took on him. So the Davidsons accommodated Rags. Each day, someone would bring Rags to Brookside in the morning and fetch him in the evening. Rags would not have to do without his daily treats and pettings.

Rags continued his daily rounds in Brookside for four years after the Davidson family moved. On September 1, 1962, following a sudden illness, Rags was put to sleep, ending a special era for the merchants and patrons of Brookside. As one neighborhood resident said in a 1960 *Kansas City Star* story on him, "Somehow you get the feeling that Rags is more than just a dog."

Catalogue: Brookside Grocers Through the Years

At the top of J.C. Nichols's list for essential businesses in his shopping centers were the grocers. Food markets have always been a fundamental element of local economies, and neighborhood groceries have been a sign of community stability since Nichols's time. They provide the most basic of human needs and serve as the place where neighbors catch up on local news. Brookside has always benefited from a strong presence of grocery stores. Starting in 1925 with its first Piggly Wiggly just east of the fire station, Brookside has been the home of seventeen different grocery stores over its history. Their presence hit a high point in 1940 when there were seven separate groceries. In the face of changing retail business models, particularly the grocery industry, Brookside is a throwback to an earlier time. The profitability of modern grocery stores demands larger square footages, more parking and better service access than Brookside can generally accommodate, and they are typically based on serving a larger geographic market. Yet Brookside's grocers have prevailed. The following is a list of Brookside grocers through the years.

- Piggly Wiggly No. 23—20 West Sixty-third Street, 1925–32.
- J.R. Jarrell—116 West Sixty-third Street, 1926.
- Bacher & Cunningham—6245 Brookside Boulevard, 1926–51.
- 63rd Street Market—116 West Sixty-third Street, 1930–34.
- Piggly Wiggly No. 66—6240 Brookside Boulevard, 1930–34. *Not only could Brookside sustain multiple grocers, but for two to three years it also sustained two separate Piggly Wiggly stores.*
- Great A&P Tea Company—314 West Sixty-third Street and 21 West Sixty-third Street, 1930–71.
- Brockhouse Brothers—116 West Sixty-third Street, 1931.
- Brookside Market—113 West Sixty-third Street, 1932–41.
- Kroger Grocery & Baking Company—12 West Sixty-third Street, 1934–54.

This and opposite page: When the city took these survey photos in 1940, Brookside had seven groceries—more than any other time in its history. The Safeway and the A&P, both on the south side of Sixty-third Street, were only a block apart. *Courtesy of the Kansas City (MO) Landmarks Commission (Kroger) and Wilborn & Associates (Milgram).*

- Milgram Food Stores No. 11—6327 Brookside Plaza, 1937–2002. *Though not destroyed in the Brookside Theatre fire, Milgram's took the opportunity of the reconstruction to expand into part of the lot the theatre had occupied. Even after the Milgram's chain was sold, the Brookside store continued to operate under the Milgram's name and was the last Milgram's store in the city when it closed in 2002.*
- Berbiglia Grocery No. 8—105 West Sixty-third Street, 1940–43. *Before it was known as a liquor store chain, Berbiglia's was a local grocery concern. After just a few years in business, this store was closed and reopened as Berbiglia's Liquor.*
- Muehlebach & Sons—6245 Brookside Boulevard, 1952–57.
- Meiner's Thriftway—21 West Sixty-third Street, 1972–91, and 14 West Sixty-second Terrace, 1992–2003.
- Safeway—14 West Sixty-second Terrace, 1975–88.
- Cosentino's Price Chopper—6327 Brookside Plaza, 2003– .
- Cosentino's Market in Brookside—14 West Sixty-second Terrace, 2005– .

Chapter 7

THE 1970S

UNEASY TIMES

Kansas City began the 1970s in an understandable state of euphoria. The Kansas City Chiefs kicked off the first month of the decade by winning the Super Bowl, and Kansas City stepped into a national spotlight that shone for the next six years. Dr. Charles Wheeler, a master of local boosterism, was elected mayor in 1971, and during his tenure, Kansas City's promotional efforts were at an all-time high. There was much to brag about. In 1972 alone, KCI Airport, Arrowhead Stadium and the Alameda Hotel on the Plaza all opened, and the revitalization of Westport and the River Quay were launched. A year later, it was Royals (now Kauffman) Stadium, Worlds of Fun and Kemper Arena that opened. Kansas City was heralding itself as the new American City, culminating in its successful bid to host the 1976 Republican Convention.

The second half of the decade could not have been more different. Cracks in the façade of civic confidence—some starting decades before—were now revealed in rapid succession. The national energy crisis slowed the local economy, which had come to depend on gas-guzzling cars in its continued suburban sprawl. The cost of every new structure was the loss of an old one. As the Truman Sports Complex was completed, the old Municipal Stadium was demolished. As Worlds of Fun opened, Fairyland Park closed for good. Where the Plaza had once been the retail home for the surrounding neighborhoods, longtime businesses were now starting to close in favor of upscale, trendy national brands. The school district was in trouble, and city infrastructure was lacking. In a crescendo of misfortune, the decade ended in a succession of tragedies—the Plaza flood in 1977, the Coates House fire in 1978 and the Kemper Arena roof collapse in 1979.

The Brookside shopping district struggled with its own issues from the very beginning of the 1970s. The organization's official correspondence from this time shows three topics of sometimes intense discussion between the association and its membership—parking, cleanliness and dues. These had all been ongoing problems in Brookside, as they are in most shopping areas. But in the 1970s, the association board often took a strident tone with its members in the memos and letters it issued in response to complaints about dues. It was increasingly difficult to get businesses to pay. The Brookside Merchants Association was operating on a thin budget. The dues structure was built upon a complicated system of assessment based on each store's location to the center of the district and its proximity to parking, all of which made the dues seem somewhat arbitrary. But the association had no enforcement mechanism, so when businesses lagged or failed to pay, it was forced to cut back on services, promotions and events.

For these and other reasons, the 1970s were also one of the highest periods of business turnover in Brookside. Many of the businesses that closed then were among Brookside's oldest and once most successful. Those closures included the Police and Fire Station (fifty-seven years), the Brookside Beauty Shop (fifty-three years), Smith Construction (fifty years), the Brookside Flower Shop (forty-four years), Parkview Drugs

Sanitation is a way of life. It is the quality of living that is expressed in the clean home, the clean farm, the clean business and industry, the clean neighborhood, the clean community. Being a way of life it must come from within the people; it is nourished by knowledge and grows as an obligation and an ideal in human relations.

PUBLIC WORKS DEPARTMENT
REFUSE COLLECTION DIVISION
17TH FLOOR, CITY HALL
KANSAS CITY 6, MISSOURI
BALTIMORE 1-1400

A homily adorned the cover of the city's brochure on sanitation, but inside there were no programs or services offered to Brookside merchants—only a list of the inculpatory ordinances. *Courtesy of the Brookside Business Association.*

(thirty-eight years), the Texaco station (thirty-seven years), Rothschild's (thirty-three years) and the A&P grocery (thirty-one years). By 1980, thirty businesses that had been in Brookside twenty years or more were gone. Brookside had experienced a changing of the guard. But one event would change the face of Brookside more than all the other struggles combined. Just about breakfast time on a frigid Sunday morning in January 1978, Harry Jacobs's Brookside Theatre Building caught fire.

The Curtain Comes Down on the Brookside Theatre

The Brookside Theatre may not have been as large or as grand as downtown theatres like the Empire or the Midland. But for its size, it was a gem. Opened in 1937, its red velvet–draped interior could hold nearly one thousand moviegoers. Like the classic movie houses, it had a freestanding box office right up to the sidewalk. Having a theatre in Brookside had been a big part of the dream of Harry Jacobs, the developer who had built it and much of Brookside's south side. Architecturally, the building was a bit of a jumble. Looking at it from the street, the theatre took up the southernmost quarter of the building. The rest was devoted to retail shops at street level and offices in the basement and on the second floor. Most of the façade of the Brookside Theatre Building, as it was known, was Colonial, and it even sported a cupola with a flagpole on top. But the theatre marquee and the massive electric sign on the roof that could be seen for blocks were more Art Deco. The theatre was the flashiest building in Brookside and a far cry from the architectural standard that J.C. Nichols had tried to establish. No matter to Harry Jacobs, however. Forty years later, looking at it in ashes, Jacobs would refer to it as "my baby."

Jacobs wanted to build a theatre, but he was a real estate man, not a movie man, so he leased it to others to operate. A corporation calling itself the Brookside Theatre Corporation (BTC) leased the facility for fifteen years. It was during these same fifteen years that the entire film industry was struggling with a series of antitrust lawsuits against the major studios, which stood accused (and ultimately convicted) of controlling everything from the distribution of movies to the price of tickets in an attempt to drive independent film producers from the market. The Brookside Theatre Corporation was caught up in the tangle. Try though it might, it had little luck securing the biggest box office draws and, as a result, typically ran so-

The Brookside Theatre Building, 1955. *The Glass Slipper* with Leslie Caron is playing, and "Cooled by Refrigeration" entices patrons. *Courtesy of the Brookside Business Association.*

called "B movies." In 1952, BTC sued the major studios as a group (which included Twentieth Century Fox, Paramount, RKO, Warner Brothers and Columbia, among others) and was awarded a judgment of $1,125,000. The studio plaintiffs appealed but were denied. Thereafter, the quality of the theatre's bookings improved, but the Brookside Theatre would always be known more as a theatre showing less popular movies.

The Brookside Theatre was an important draw for the district and the focal point of many promotions by the Brookside Merchants Association. In 1960, the lobby was transformed into a French sidewalk café for *Can-Can*. Bathing beauties arrived via antique cars for *Those Magnificent Men in Their Flying Machines* (1965), and American Indian dancers performed in the streets for *Two Rode Together* (1961). Perhaps the most elaborate promotion, and in retrospect one of the strangest, was for the 1961 redistribution of *Gone With the Wind*. Brookside's advertising in the *Wednesday Magazine* promoted the event as a "celebration" of the centennial of the start of the Civil War.

Because of its antitrust battles with the major film corporations, the Brookside Theatre wasn't always able to run the most popular movies, but it offered plenty of family-friendly films. *Courtesy of Sun Publications.*

An organ grinder's monkey entertains Bea Mann, secretary to the merchants' association, and businessman Roy Hill as part of the street entertainment before the Kansas City premiere of *Can-Can* at the Brookside Theatre, 1960. *Courtesy of the Brookside Business Association.*

The promotion lasted a week and included the usual window displays, and Brookside patrons voted on their favorite Brookside employee to be the "Southern Belle" of the premiere.

As a movie house, the Brookside Theatre was struggling as it came into the 1970s. Moviegoers wanted big suburban multiplexes with large screens and high-tech sound systems. The theatre played its last movie in 1976. In 1977, there were plans underway to turn the vacant theatre into a venue for live music, a venture that had met with mixed reactions from the neighborhoods. The music hall was scheduled to open in February 1978.

Later, it would be determined that the fire started in Nick's Bar-B-Q on the Theatre Building's ground floor. The first call came in at 8:30 a.m. on Sunday morning, January 29. It could hardly have happened on a worse day. There were four major fires in the city that weekend, including the horrific Coates House fire downtown. The fire department's capacity was stretched to its limits. The situation was made worse by the five-degree temperatures, causing water to freeze not only on the streets and buildings but also to the firefighters themselves and rendering one truck inoperable. The crews fought the blaze from the street, from ladder trucks and from the roofs of nearby buildings. There would be two more calls for additional units before the fire was conquered about midday, crowding Brookside with seventy-five firefighters and more than a dozen vehicles.

The damage was tremendous, and the only bright spot was that no one had been seriously injured. Property loss was nearly complete. Altogether, some twenty businesses were displaced. Almost immediately, other Brookside merchants helped out. Merli Jewelry moved to temporary space in the Plaza Bank. The Kellogg Hair Salon moved in with the John Ryan Salon. Others found space in Harry Jacobs's building across the street. Baskin-Robbins Ice Cream moved to its present location at Sixty-third and Wornall Road.

Ironically, of all the parts of the building damaged by the fire, the Brookside Theatre sustained the least amount of damage. The lobby was destroyed, but the auditorium was largely intact. And initially, eighty-eight-year-old Harry Jacobs was determined to rebuild. He planned to reconstruct the building just as it had been. He believed there was enough left—the outer walls and other structural elements—to make the project work. But it was not to be. Nearly a year later, the city finally declared the building unsafe and ordered it to be razed. Jacobs tried to fight at first but, in the end, saw the futility of it. It took another two years of complicated negotiations among the various property owners on Brookside Plaza, but in 1980, Milgram's opened an expanded store at the south end of the block, abutting a smaller lower-level office space that

Harry Jacobs built as his own offices—the nicest, he said at the time, that he had ever had. He was happy to have fewer tenants to manage, and the grocery store was beautiful and modern, a wonderful asset to the Brookside Shops. But the cost had been great, including businesses that would never return, like Norman Hoyt's Studio, photographer of record for all of Brookside's major events, and the Brookside Theatre Barber Shop, which had stood beside the theatre's entry since it first opened. There would never be another movie house in Brookside. And the beautiful—if garish—lighted "Brookside Theatre" sign that had sat on the roof of the Brookside Theatre Building was gone for good.

THE DIME STORES

Regardless of any uncertainty the Brookside Shops might have been experiencing in the 1970s, there was one store that served as a bastion of stability and has continued to do so since—the Dime Store at 314 West Sixty-third Street. There is no other store that has ever been as fondly remembered, as frequently visited or as much a barometer of the health of Brookside as that simple, unassuming variety store that has operated in the same space for nearly seventy years.

In 1941, the Ben Franklin Variety Store moved into the A&P grocery store's first Brookside location, after A&P moved three blocks east. Ben Franklin was a relatively new company then, having started under that name in 1927. It had a unique business model for the time—it franchised the stores and served primarily as a wholesaler. While the model proved successful for decades, in Brookside the Ben Franklin store lasted only a couple of years. It was Laning's Dime Store by 1944. Josephine Laning was the owner, and the store then followed the typical layout and merchandising of the five-and-dime, with long counters behind which stood most of the store's inventory. Clerks stood at the counters ready to assist customers with their orders. On displays scattered throughout the store were all the small sundry items every household needed—shoe polish, work gloves and tools for the men; cooking utensils, sewing notions and gift wrap for the ladies; toy trucks, balloons and penny candy for the children. With its something-for-everyone offerings, its friendly and familiar staff and its propensity for being someplace you were sure to run into someone you knew, Laning's Dime Store quickly became the heart of the Brookside community.

Eventually, the long counters were replaced by a central station near the front, but other than that, the store would change little over the years.

Briefly beginning as a Ben Franklin store (1941–43), the shop at 314 West Sixty-third Street operated as Laning's Dime Store for nearly twenty years before Ernest Arfsten bought it in 1963. *Courtesy of WHMC KC106n294.*

Even when merchandise had become relics of times gone by—things like clothespins, potato mashers and shaving brushes—they were still in stock at the Dime Store. Many employees also remained for years. One in particular, Ernest Arfsten, would be there nearly from the beginning and would help ensure the longevity of the Dime Store.

Arfsten was a true retailer. He started out working for the local grocery store in his hometown of Moorehead, Minnesota, and had worked for the S.S. Kresge Company in Chicago for several years when, in 1944, he was enticed to move to Kansas City and manage the Dime Store. He came here with a wife and two children. His son, Bob, was just a teenager then, attending Southwest High School and working part time for his dad. Though it would be another twenty years before Arfsten would buy the store from Laning's estate, from that time forward it was effectively the Arfstens' store. It would be their winning ways with the customers and the other merchants that would guarantee the Dime Store's place in Brookside. That, and the wooden floors.

Wooden floors were a standard part of the design when Nichols built the Brookside Shops. At one time, every store would have had wooden floors.

But over the years, as other materials came into favor, the wood disappeared, replaced by linoleum or carpet. But in the Dime Store, they remained. Over the years, the familiar creak became an evocative sense memory for virtually anyone who had ever shopped there, synonymous with the store itself. A 1973 fire caused extensive damage to the store, and while there was never a question about reopening, there were plenty of questions from longtime customers about whether the wooden floors would return. The Arfstens considered changes, but the customers would have none of it, and the Nichols Company replaced the wooden floors.

Ernest's son, Bob, came to work at the Dime Store full time in 1954, after a stint in the service. He was, like his father, a natural at this homespun sort of retail. He kept up with the lives of his customers, truly enjoyed helping them around the store and never fussed because children played in the aisles. Ten years later, his father bought the store and continued to work there until the 1970s. But by all accounts, once Bob came to the store full time, it was clear the store was his. They belonged together.

By the 1990s, the store was as popular and beloved as it had always been, but there were small signs of stress on the business. The dime store as a retail idea was outmoded. In the wake of larger retailers— some of which had started out in the five-and-dime business themselves—small variety stores struggled. And even with rents based on a percentage of sales, costs continued to rise. It was increasingly difficult

Bob Arfsten took over the Dime Store from his father and became a Brookside fixture and favorite until his death in 2002. *Courtesy of Sun Publications.*

to show a profit. But Bob Arfsten stayed even after the shop began to show no profit at all. He stayed because he believed his friends—his customers, his employees and the other merchants—needed him and, even more, needed the Dime Store, to keep Brookside as Brookside. That need became critical in 1997, when the J.C. Nichols Company was purchased by Highwoods Properties, an out-of-town developer. The status of the Dime Store—*Would it stay open? Would it be replaced by a major retailer?*—became the litmus test for the health of Brookside.

Ultimately, it wouldn't be the purchase of the Nichols Company or even the state of the retail industry that would most threaten the future of the Dime Store. On a quiet Saturday morning in November 2002, Bob Arfsten passed away in his Brookside neighborhood home. He was seventy-two and died of natural causes. The news hit the city hard and Brookside harder. Spontaneous memorials appeared in front of the shop by midday. Generations of customers came by to console and be consoled by the staff. Among the Brookside merchants, the grief was particularly strong. With the grief came a resurgence of the old worries. Bob had no family in the area. The fate of the Dime Store was unknown. That it might possibly close could be the opportunity the new owners had been looking for to overhaul the very character of Brookside.

Eventually, it was determined that an out-of-town niece was Bob's only heir. She tried but was unsuccessful in her first attempts to sell the business. For more than three years after Arfsten's death, former employees and family representatives tried to keep the business operating. During that time, the ownership of the former Nichols property had returned to local hands, hands willing to help keep the Dime Store open. But in June 2006, for the first time in sixty-six years, the doors closed, and there was no Dime Store in Brookside.

For six months, the store stood locked. Peering through the windows into the darkened shop was like looking at a museum piece—a nostalgic view of the way life used to be and a sad reminder of how it might never be again. Then suddenly, though not entirely out of nowhere, a buyer appeared. Fifi Wiedeman was another longtime Brooksider who grew up a Dime Store regular. She knew Bob Arfsten well and had talked to him over the years about slowly buying him out of the business, while still keeping him involved in the operation. Bob would seem interested, but the bargain was never struck. Once it was clear the last operators couldn't make a go of it, she pitched the idea one more time. This time, she was successful.

Six months later, the Dime Store reopened, christened now the New Dime Store. Wiedeman considered it an apt name, for it captured both the tradition and the improvements. The store finally had computerization. With the help of her husband, Reeves, an architect, the space was redesigned to retain much of the old feel but with a fresh look. The wooden floors, of course, remained.

The legacy of Bob Arfsten's love for the Brookside Shops was integrated into the renovation of Brookside Court Park in 2008. The park, on the southeast corner of Sixty-third Street and Brookside Boulevard, was updated in a cooperative project of the city's Parks Department, the Brookside Business Association and friends of Bob Arfsten's who raised money to dedicate the park in his honor. Fittingly, the memorial includes a patio space for friends to congregate and, in the center, a small area of wooden floor.

CATALOGUE: BEST BROOKSIDE BUSINESS NAMES

In its ninety-year history, there have been more than one thousand individual businesses in Brookside. On that long roster, there are many businesses whose tenure was brief and whose historical significance has yet to be learned. Yet their names alone evoke a smile—for their cleverness, their uniqueness or the simple fact that they seem to capture the essence of a particular bygone time.

- Kane's School of Expression and Dancing—6247 Brookside Boulevard, 1931–32.
- Monkey Cleaners and Dyers—6239 Brookside Plaza, 1931–47.
- The Darling Frock Shop—6247 Brookside Plaza, 1933–34.
- Mrs. Stover's Bungalow Candies—6306 Brookside Plaza, 1935–42.
- Shop Beautiful—320 West Sixty-third Street, 1936– .
- Melody Lane (records)—126 West Sixty-third Street, 1941–43.
- The Elizabeth Corset Salon—6315 Brookside Plaza, 1942–49.
- Marguerite's Gowns of Distinction—6305 Brookside Plaza, 1945–46.
- Lullaby House (infants' wear)—6306 Brookside Plaza, 1950–52.
- Nukem Products Corp. (manufacturers' representative)—121 West Sixty-third Street, 1952–57.
- The Toddle House (restaurant)—9 West Sixty-third Street, 1952–72.
- Shears and Tears (beauty salon)—6313 Brookside Plaza, 1953–57.
- Hogerty's Pink Poodle (bar)—12 West Sixty-third Street, 1966–68.
- Motivators (ladies' undergarments—wholesale)—6315 Brookside Plaza, 1966–68.
- Bridge a La Verne Bridge Club—6330 Brookside Plaza, 1967–69.
- Poor Richard's Candle Wasters (bar)—6330 Brookside Plaza, 1970–78.

Chapter 8

THE 1980S

THE MAIN EVENTS

After the troubling declines of the late 1970s, it would be the mid-1980s before the country felt back on its feet again. In Kansas City, recovery was buoyed yet again by a sports triumph—the Royals' World Series championship in 1985. Brookside, like the rest of the city, went wild that night. As they watched the game on television, the ecstatic fans inside Charlie Hooper's Bar & Grille could be heard two blocks away. After the win, parades of cars honked as they circled through the streets of Brookside, and as they streamed out of restaurants and bars, people filled the streets. Brookside stayed up until dawn.

By 1985, Brookside was gaining a reputation it hadn't enjoyed in a while—as a place where things happen. The merchants' association had been in a rut over the past decade. Its promotions were still successful but a little less so each year, and since the theatre had burned down, events were on a smaller scale. After serving the Brookside Merchants Association for more than two decades, executive secretary Bea Mann had retired. This presented an opportunity for a new approach, some merchants felt. They urged Virginia Kellogg to apply for the job. Kellogg and her husband, Everett, had operated several hair salons in Brookside for years. Virginia was known for her energy and her enthusiasm for Brookside. The board hired her in 1981.

Soon after, the association began publishing a new newsletter, the *Brookside Lamplighter*. The quarterly was more newsy than news-filled, with heavy emphasis on advertising and highlighting Brookside businesses. But it was mailed to all the area residences, something which had not been done since

A metal Christmas tree built by Everett Kellogg of Salon Kellogg and John Malang of Malang's House of Design decorated the Brookside shopping district for the holidays in the 1970s. *Courtesy of the Brookside Business Association.*

publication of Nichols's *Country Club Bulletin* fifty years earlier. It also had a complete listing of all the businesses in every issue and was heavily distributed throughout the shops, making it the perfect shopping guide.

Some traditional events, like the Sidewalk Sale, continued, but Brookside began introducing new ways to attract people. Some events were tried but for various reasons didn't last. "Brookside in Bloom" was introduced in the early 1980s to draw attention to the many plantings and flowerboxes in Brookside in the spring. "Octoberfest," begun later in the early 1990s, invited children to come out to the pumpkin patch in costume. Both lasted only a few years. But the 1980s produced two events and a promotion that have had a lasting effect on Brookside's image—the St. Patrick's Day Warm-up Parade, the Brookside Art Annual and the restoration of the gaslights.

THE ST. PATRICK'S DAY WARM-UP PARADE

Technically, Brookside had its first St. Patrick's Day parade in the 1970s. Longtime and former merchants still remember a St. Patrick's Day in the mid-1970s when the proprietor and patrons of Hogerty's tavern formed an impromptu parade around the district, no doubt inspired by the origins of the downtown St. Patrick's Day Parade. But in 1981, Brookside decided to make it official, although with a twist.

The concept for the Warm-up Parade arose from the idea to get a jump on the growing popularity of the downtown parade, by now a significant event on Kansas City's holiday calendar. Kellogg saw St. Patrick's Day as a natural fit with the Brookside area, owing to the large number of families who claimed (rightly or not) some Irish heritage. By making it the "warm-up" parade, Brookside would have the distinction of kicking off the city's St. Patrick's Day celebrations.

Initially, the parade was staged in the parking lot by the tennis courts on Brookside Boulevard. Then it wound around Meyer Boulevard, heading north on Brookside Plaza and then east on Sixty-third Street. Those first years, the participants were largely children—school groups, scout troops or just a gaggle of neighborhood kids and their parents. A car was pressed into service to chauffer the dignitary who served as grand marshal. That was all. According to Kellogg, the whole parade couldn't have lasted more than thirty minutes. In one of those early years, a local television station arrived to film the parade

Participants often exceeded spectators in the early St. Patrick's Day Warm-up Parades. Cars were still parked on Brookside Plaza as the parade goes by. *Courtesy of the Brookside Business Association.*

By the 1990s, the St. Patrick's Day Warm-up Parade had lengthened its route and grown to fill Sixty-third Street. *Courtesy of the Brookside Business Association.*

just as it was ending. "I told them to wait a few minutes," Kellogg recalled, "and we just sent the parade around a second time." In just a few years, the parade grew too large for the Brookside Plaza route. Today, the route stages on Brookside Road just south of the district, comes north on Wornall Road to Sixty-third Street and then east to its conclusion at Main Street.

The identity of that first grand marshal is apparently lost to history. But over the years, the parade has featured local dignitaries of all stripes as grand marshals, including most Kansas City mayors, city council members and other elected officials and a few of Brookside's longtime tenants—each proud to be Irish for one day. Later years also saw the parade committee naming a "Mr. and Mrs. Irish," a couple who have been involved in Brookside for a long time. The number of entrants grew from an estimated twenty the first year to more than one hundred by the time the association had to limit entries. Starting in the late 1980s, entries were judged in several categories, including best float, best theme and best music. Even with its modest beginnings, the Brookside St. Patrick's Day Warm-up Parade was recognized as a success. The new leadership of the merchants' association proved adept at attracting media attention and support of public officials. It was a perfect first step for Brookside, but soon there was an even bigger event in the works.

Local dignitaries are a fixture at the St. Patrick's Day Warm-up Parade. *From left*: Senator Harry Wiggins (in hat), City Councilmen Bob Llewellen, Emanuel Cleaver II, Frank Palermo, Chuck Weber, Kathryn Shields and others are coached in their roles in the late 1980s. *Courtesy of the Brookside Business Association.*

THE BROOKSIDE ART ANNUAL

Brookside may have been built first, but it was the Country Club Plaza that started the local tradition of art fairs in 1931. Westport held its first in 1979 as part of its revitalization efforts. Virginia Kellogg and other Brookside merchants believed an art fair could work in Brookside. Kellogg started trying to convince merchants to support the event almost from the moment she took over management of the business association.

Unfortunately, many merchants were unconvinced. Some doubted it would be a draw—after all, weren't there already enough art fairs in midtown? Others cited the fact that an art fair never seemed to draw customers to the stores. Others said the association couldn't afford the expense of an art fair. Virginia Kellogg was not to be dissuaded, but she was willing to compromise. The compromise centered on what the more traditional Brookside merchants still believed was a tried-and-true success—window displays. In August 1983, Brookside had its first art fair. Billed as a "Window Shopping Art Exhibit," the work of some thirty local artists was displayed in the front windows

On Saturday, August Twenty-seventh

Come take a leisurely stroll through the Brookside "Window Shopping Art Exhibit and Sale."

Artworks displayed will represent some of Kansas City's best known artists such as Barbara Burnett, Rod Cofran, Bob Holloway, and Margaret Parish along with over 30 other well known artists from the Brookside community.

"The Brookside merchants have created an uncrowded and relaxing atmosphere for patrons of the Brookside Shops to shop and sample some of Kansas City's finest artists' works," says Virginia Kellogg, secretary of the Brookside Merchants Association.

The "Window Shopping Art Exhibit and Sale" will be for *one day only* at the Brookside Shops, 63rd and Brookside Boulevard.

A simple flyer was the only promotion for the first attempt at an art fair in Brookside, where displays where limited to shop windows. *Courtesy of the Brookside Business Association.*

of participating shops. Bob Holloway, whose line drawings of whole city districts often appeared in print and advertising at the time, was one of the featured artists, and he created a popular print of Brookside for the occasion. Many of the participants were instructors from the Kansas City Art Institute or professional artists who lived in the neighborhoods around Brookside. The day of the fair, some artists worked *en plein air*, painting the street scenes of Brookside as if it were the Left Bank of the Seine. The art exhibit lasted only one Saturday. It was not an unqualified success, but the public reaction was sufficiently favorable to convince the Brookside merchants that there was something to this art fair business after all.

From then on, Kellogg pushed for a full-fledged art fair in the streets of Brookside. To pull that off would take considerably more planning than anything Brookside had put on to date—so much planning, in fact, that it would be the spring of 1986 before Brookside would have its first true art

Tents are readied for setup on Brookside Boulevard between Sixty-third Street and Meyer Boulevard for the first Brookside Art Annual held on the streets of Brookside. *Courtesy of the Brookside Business Association.*

The Art Annual has grown to accommodate more artists, set up here in the south parking lot. *Courtesy of the Brookside Business Association.*

fair. Kellogg and her committee members met with folks from the Plaza and Westport Art Fairs to learn the secrets. A budget had to be created and funding planned for. Most importantly, the Brookside group wanted to draw from a national pool of artists. Those artists were typically scheduling their trips to art fairs all around the country a year in advance. It took every bit of 1984 and 1985 to plan that first art fair or, as it came to be called, the Brookside Art Annual.

Except for its growth, little about the Art Annual has changed in the last twenty-five years. Since 1986, it has always been held the first weekend in May. From the beginning, the activity centered under large tents set up along Brookside Boulevard, blocked off from traffic between Sixty-third Street and Meyer Boulevard. The brightly colored tents used in the early years were eventually replaced by white tents, which provided a more flattering light in which to view the artists' works. The first year the tents accommodated 122 artists. The event grew so popular with the public and artists alike that it soon expanded into the parking lot to the east of Brookside Boulevard to a capacity of nearly 150 artists. Brookside merchants continue to participate in a variety of ways, including the support of the awards given to artists in various media.

Best of all, the Art Annual was a bonanza for the Brookside Business Association. Not only did the fair attract large numbers of people, but it also significantly raised Brookside's profile both locally and nationally. By 2000, it was being heralded as one of the top five art fairs in the country, which, combined with the even more widely known Plaza Art Fair, put Kansas City squarely on the national art fair scene. Further, it turned out to be a significant source of revenue for the district, more than enough to cover the costs of the fair and provide the association with a tidy sum for other promotion and advertising throughout the year. The Brookside Art Annual helped bring a level of financial stability that the organization had struggled to maintain for nearly twenty years and cemented Brookside's position as one of Kansas City's destination districts.

CATALOGUE: THE GASLIGHTS, SYMBOLS OF BROOKSIDE

It's uncertain when the gaslights first appeared in Brookside, exactly how many there were or where they were originally placed. Photos of the earliest years don't show any lamps at all. Photos from the early 1940s show lamps on Sixty-third Street and Brookside Plaza, placed at regular intervals along the

This page: Brookside has restored seventeen of its signature gas lamps, including this one converted to solar power on Brookside Plaza. *Courtesy of the author.*

sidewalks, apparently more utilitarian than decorative. These first gaslights were of a different style than those later installed. A single cylindrical globe with a black cap sat atop the tall black standard. It is generally assumed that the present-day lamps were installed in the late 1940s or early 1950s at the instigation of the Nichols Company. These gaslights feature a trinity of lamps with small eagles as finials on the tops.

The lamps burned brightly until the energy crisis of 1973, when the government urged cutbacks in consumption wherever possible. As a cost-saving measure, the Brookside lamps were extinguished. In 1982, twelve of the gaslights were refurbished and ceremonially lit for the Christmas holiday, a tradition that stood for several years. In 1989, the Brookside Business Association started a campaign to relight the lamps year-round and add three more lamps. When these second-generation gaslights were installed, the gas bill was assigned to one of the businesses adjacent to each lamp. The late '80s strategy was to have Brookside businesses sponsor each gaslight, at an estimated cost at the time of twenty-one dollars per month. If a business couldn't afford that, it could sponsor a single lantern on the fixture for seven dollars per month. Through the campaign, Brookside received sponsorship for twelve lamps. Over the years, some of the supporting businesses closed or left the area, leaving the gaslights without sponsorship. Others fell into disrepair, and service for the lamp fixtures was increasingly difficult to find. Eventually, only a few of the gaslights continued to operate. In the late 1990s and early 2000s, another attempt was made to refurbish the lights. With the advent of the Brookside Community Improvement District (CID) in 2005, there was some limited funding again for maintenance and repair. The CID also explored the option of switching the lights to solar power, and eventually two were converted. The conversions proved costly, however, and the technology additions detracted from the gaslights' appearance.

The gaslights continue to be maintained, although some have been lost due to inappropriate placement, damage done by vehicles or improvements to sidewalks and buildings. The following is an inventory of the gaslights' positions—both original and current. In addition to these, it is generally thought that gaslights were once also located at Sixty-third and Main (southwest corner) and Meyer Boulevard and Brookside Plaza (northwest corner).

- Sixty-third Street and Wornall Road (northeast corner)—*At a prominent entrance to Brookside and in the corner of a small parking lot, this light is one of two that has been converted to solar power.*

- Sixty-third Street and Brookside Boulevard (all corners)—*Each of the four corners of the central intersection in Brookside sports a gaslight.*
- Sixty-second Terrace and Brookside Boulevard (east and west)—*Near the entrance to the service alley on the west side, the base of a gaslight is still visible. This light was moved to a new location on Sixty-second Terrace in approximately 2005. On the west side of the street, near what was once the entrance to the Nichols Company's Brookside office, another original lamp stands. This one bears a plaque indicating it was adopted by the Nichols Company during the 1989 campaign.*
- Sixty-second Terrace (between Brookside Boulevard and Brookside Plaza)—*This lamp was moved from its original location on the west side of Brookside Boulevard. It bears a new plaque in memory of Wanda Davidson.*
- Sixty-second Terrace and Brookside Plaza (east and west)—*At the time of this writing, these gaslights have been temporarily removed for repairs.*
- Sixty-third Street and Brookside Plaza (northeast and southwest corners)—*Another prominent Brookside intersection once featured four lamps; the one on the northwest corner has been permanently removed in favor of the placement of Brookside's living Holiday Tree. The gaslight on the southeast corner was removed during major repairs to the sidewalk in recent years. The lamp on the southwest corner is the second of the solar conversions.*
- Sixty-third Street and Baltimore Avenue (east and west)—*Two of the best examples of working lamps sit here on the south side of Sixty-third Street. The one on the east side of Baltimore still bears the plaque of its sponsor, Meiner's Thriftway, which occupied the adjacent building at the time of the gaslight campaign. Across the street, the lamp bears the sponsorship plaque of Commerce Bank.*
- Sixty-third Street and Main (northwest corner)—*Another prominent Brookside entrance, this lamp bears no plaque.*
- Sixty-second Terrace and Main (southwest corner)—*This lamp was removed in recent years to accommodate renovations to the building at 7 West Sixty-second Terrace.*
- Meyer Boulevard and Brookside Plaza (northeast corner)—*This lamp was removed in recent years to accommodate landscape improvements.*

Chapter 9

THE 1990S

THE END OF THE NICHOLS ERA

As the 1990s began, what had been lauded as the '80s real estate boom was now being labeled a "real estate bubble." Too many speculators had artificially inflated values, and now all that speculation was crumbling. Nationally, the impacts were significant, but in Kansas City they were profound in a particular way. For the first time in its eighty-year history, the venerated Nichols Company seemed vulnerable.

The Brookside Business Association had made great strides over the last decade, emerging more energized than ever. Distinct in its own way as both Westport and the Plaza had become, it competed with them as a unique and popular local destination. And even though the Nichols Company now had numerous shopping districts in its stable—Prairie Village, Corinth and Red Bridge, among others—Brookside still believed in its status with the company, owing to its heritage as the oldest. Now those assumptions, and in fact the very future of the Brookside Shops, were up in the air. In 1988, the Nichols family effectively sold the Nichols Company to its employees, through a mechanism known as an employee ownership stock plan. The sale was initiated by management, at the time led by Lynn McCarthy, who had succeeded Miller Nichols in 1984, though Nichols continued as a board member. McCarthy had been with the company since 1958, starting out as an accountant. He was a trusted member of the higher echelon and the principal engineer of the buyout.

By all accounts, the $100 million or so price tag paid for the company by the employee plan was high—too high, it seemed, once the real estate market started to turn. Still, the Nichols Company was in an enviable and almost

A contemporary iron gate at Brookside Real Estate on Sixty-third Street honors the traditions of Brookside. *Courtesy of the author.*

unique position within the real estate industry. For most of its life, it had operated relatively debt free, in an industry that was at the time addicted to debt. Locally, everyone assumed the buyout might stretch the company for a while, but it would certainly remain whole. But in recent years, the Nichols Company had started to expand outside Kansas City. In particular, a venture into the Florida commercial real estate market proved expensive, requiring Nichols to take on additional debt. When the bubble burst, even more money was leveraged trying to keep the project afloat—a $20 million retail center had been built, and by 1991, there were no tenants.

Then the Nichols Company did something that would have at one time seemed unthinkable. It secured a $45 million line of credit with Frank Morgan's Merchants Bank and used the Country Club Plaza as collateral. Nichols's flagship property was at risk, even as Nichols's management continued to proclaim the move as just one of many debt-restructuring steps it was strategically taking. Its claims were unconvincing to many. Doubts were compounded by a series of shareholder lawsuits, all of which claimed improper actions by management. The project in Florida grew shakier, and Nichols had to pledge additional investment. Quarter after quarter, the Nichols Company reported declines in earnings. Then, the Fairway Shops, another of the Country Club District shopping centers, was put up for sale, raising speculation about the future of that area. The Nichols Company, a Kansas City real estate institution, had gone from rock solid stability to a questionable future in just one year.

The Nichols Company's woes continued through the rest of the decade. Lawsuits mounted. Debt restructuring continued. The company divested itself of some properties for which it had long had development plans. McCarthy, who would later plead guilty to charges of fraud, was ousted by the board. The Nichols Company struggled with its direction from then on. A series of management changes were announced. One was particularly problematic for many merchants, including those in Brookside. In 1997, the Nichols Company acquired a local property management firm to manage the Brookside, Corinth and Prairie Village shops. Two years before, Nichols had already closed the management office it had occupied in Brookside since 1976. Almost immediately, the Brookside merchants began to have problems. Tenants were having difficulty getting anyone to respond to their interest in renewing leases. The neglect may have been simple oversight or poor management, but in Brookside some tenants started to feel suspicious. Perhaps this meant the new management was trying to force old tenants out.

Late in 1997, the answer to the future of the Nichols Company came. It was what everyone feared. The Nichols Company was sold. Worst of all, from the perspective of local tenants, it was sold to an out-of-town firm, one that didn't have any track record in retail. Speculation began almost immediately that the "outlying shopping centers," as J.C. Nichols had first called them, would be overhauled. In November 1999, the new owner, Highwoods Properties of North Carolina, announced it was accepting offers on some of its other local properties, including three closely associated with Brookside—the Colonial, Crestwood and Romanelli Shops. Still, as the decade came to a close, Highwoods promised that it had no plans to sell the Brookside Shops. Few in Brookside felt reassured.

THE *WEDNESDAY MAGAZINE*, BROOKSIDE'S HOMETOWN PAPER

The *Country Club District Bulletin* was one of J.C. Nichols's first services to his neighborhoods. Nichols felt so strongly that the district's success was tied to good communication with the residents that he not only published the bulletin but also reportedly wrote much of it himself in the early days. However, the bulletin was also one of the first services jettisoned during the cost-cutting measures of the Depression. Perhaps that was the opportunity Ernest Brown recognized when he started the *Wednesday Magazine* in 1937.

Ernest Brown, founder of the *Wednesday Magazine*, Brookside's "hometown" newspaper. *Courtesy of Sun Publications.*

Brown was sixty-four at the time. He had always been in the newspaper business, as either a printer or publisher, and for a while had published a small newspaper called the *Kansas City World*. He had already retired once, but eleven years later he decided to start the *Wednesday Magazine*, as a hobby, he claimed later. His first market was the Brookside Shops, and the publication's modest four-page spread was designed specifically to promote businesses to the residents of the Country Club District, with an initial circulation of four thousand. The *Wednesday*, as it came to be called, quickly expanded with the growing population of south Kansas City, its initial market. By the early 1960s, circulation reached twenty thousand. By the mid-1960s, it was up to thirty thousand. Commercial areas were quickly added to its advertisers' list—Waldo, Prairie Village and Red Bridge. As the population in Johnson County grew, the paper added Leawood and Ward Parkway and then turned east to include the new Landing Shopping Center.

In 1966, the *Wednesday* made Brookside its headquarters when it moved into offices in the Brookside Plaza Building. The newspaper's format was simple and folksy. Regular features included "This Week's Chuckles," "This World of Ours" and "100 Years Ago." There were want ads, comics and crosswords, all the features of a regular paper. By now the paper was twenty-four pages, and each shopping area had a two-page advertising spread, buffeted by small articles about the area itself. The Brookside Merchants Association featured a "Merchant of the Week" column to promote its businesses. Focus was on the personal life of the merchants, and the piece always included mention of the owner's family, hobbies, affiliations and the nickname by which everyone in Brookside knew him. The *Wednesday* was the place to read which Southwest High student had won the recent Brookside window display contest, what festivities were planned around the shops for the upcoming holiday and what would be playing at the Brookside Theatre. But the *Wednesday* was more than just an advertising piece. It was adept at covering stories of local interest, sometimes before they caught the attention of the larger papers. Such was the case in the late 1950s with the planned Country Club Freeway. And it frequently featured the work of Brookside photographer Norman Hoyt, providing an important visual inventory of Brookside over the years.

Once, however, its Brookside connection was no help in covering a breaking story. In the 1960s, a bank robbery occurred at Plaza Savings & Loan, directly across the street from the *Wednesday*'s second-story offices on Brookside Plaza. The paper was under deadline, however, and everyone was too busy to notice the commotion outside the window until the incident was over. The story wouldn't appear until the next issue. To its credit, the *Wednesday* good-naturedly reported its gaff as part of the story.

Ernest Brown retired from the paper in 1955 but continued as editor emeritus and as a frequent poetry contributor. His son Alpha, his only child and an attorney practicing in Brookside, took over. Eventually, Al's son Richard would take over from him, and the paper continued as a family endeavor. Finally, through a series of media company buyouts, the *Wednesday* became part of the News-Press & Gazette Co. of St. Joseph. Grouped with NP&G's Sun Publications, the newspaper remerged as the *Wednesday Sun* in 2006. It continues to serve the Brookside area to this day.

HOME-BASED BROOKSIDE: THE HOUSE CONVERSIONS

Only a generation or two ago, people often ran businesses out of their homes with little or no notice. Particularly in areas where commercial and residential areas adjoin, the practice was common. All types of businesses operated this way. Trades and crafts like mechanics, dressmakers and beauticians were prevalent; so, too, were professionals like doctors and lawyers. To some extent, the growing number of small shopping areas like Brookside made the practice less common, with their small, affordable spaces. And neighborhoods like those in the Country Club District also played their part in the decline of home-based businesses. Such businesses were often considered nuisances, and eventually zoning laws restricted the ability of a person to work out of the home.

Yet these businesses have always been part of the Brookside landscape and have played a part in aiding in its development and maintaining its character.

Frisbie Realty Company converted this house on Sixty-second Terrace to its offices in the late 1930s. *Courtesy of the Kansas City (MO) Landmarks Commission.*

Even though the Nichols Company had developed all the Brookside area north of Sixty-third Street, there were houses converted to businesses on the north side of Sixty-second Terrace until the late 1940s, including attorney Edna Sperry, piano teacher Amy Winning and the Frisbie Realty Company. The first building on that street constructed exclusively for commercial purposes was the relocated Brookside Garage, built in 1949.

In Brookside, the greatest concentration of these businesses was, and continues to be, along Main Street, Brookside's eastern border. Because such businesses do not typically draw high levels of traffic, they can often coexist nicely with residential properties. Interior decorators, real estate agents, photographers, dressmakers are among the more common types of businesses that have operated successfully along Main Street. Main Street is home to one of Brookside's oldest tenants, Noah's Ark, a veterinary clinic, operating since 1971. Among the more unique tenants on Main Street was the Transcendental Meditation Center, at the southeast corner of Sixty-third and Main Streets from 1985 to 1995.

In the earlier days, there were also houses that served as businesses along Baltimore and Wyandotte (now Brookside Plaza). The last holdout

The house at 6333 Brookside Plaza had served as dental offices for nearly two decades when it was demolished in the 1960s to create more parking. *Courtesy of Kansas City (MO) Landmarks Commission.*

from that era was the house at 6333 Brookside Plaza. In 1935, as Harry Jacobs was just beginning construction of the Brookside Theatre Building, Dr. Harry Allshouse Jr., a physician, and Dr. Elizabeth Hulse, a dentist, opened their practices in the small red brick converted bungalow. Another dentist, Dr. Wayne White, joined them in 1945. Hulse and Allshouse left shortly thereafter, but Dr. White would remain there as the former house's last tenant until 1964. The house was torn down to create additional parking. After the Brookside Theatre fire in 1978, the adjacent Milgram's grocery expanded into its former parking lot, and the 6333 lot became the store's parking.

Catalogue: Brookside Gas Stations Then and Now

Brookside was built with the car in mind. J.C. Nichols knew he was building homes for the emerging automotive generation. The first building constructed in Brookside was a filling station, and one of the last was for the Faddis Motor Company at Sixty-second Terrace and Main Street.

Between 1938 and 1960, Brookside supported five different filling stations, occupying some of the district's most prominent locations. The Brookside Standard Station (later Amoco Oil), that first station built by Nichols, still holds the distinction as the longest running of the five, from 1914 to 1999. A close second is the still-operating Phillips 66 station on the northwest corner of Sixty-third and Main Streets, open since 1928. The converted filling stations, auto repair shops and car dealerships have been transformed into some of Brookside's most interesting spaces. Some have, remarkably, retained much of the look of the old buildings, while others are nearly unrecognizable in their current form. A summary of Brookside's automotive meccas of the past and present, and their incarnations over the years, is given here.

- Brookside Standard Station, Sixty-second Terrace and Brookside Boulevard, 1914–99. *The first and longest-running Brookside filling station was for years known simply as "the Brookside Station." Between 1940 and 1972 it operated as Brown's Brookside Standard. Between 1989 and its closing in 1999, it was operated by Ken West, who owned several Amoco stations in the area. After BKS Real Estate acquired it in 2005 as part of its purchase of the original Nichols buildings, the renovation was one of its first projects. The exterior retained much of the original look as it was transformed into the Roasterie Café, the only retail location for locally owned Roasterie Coffee, which was started in the basement of owner Danny O'Neill's Brookside home in 1993.*
- Brookside Garage, 104 West Sixth-third Street, and later 18 West Sixty-second Terrace, 1921–60. *More than a simple filling station, the Nichols Company built this full-service garage to entice the owners to move from the south side of Sixty-third Street, near Baltimore Avenue. Originally, it was a Skelly Oil station.*
- Brookside 66 Service, Sixty-third and Main Streets, 1928– . *For the first two years of operation, this station was affiliated with the Winters Oil Company. It became a Phillips station in 1930. It is the last operating service station in Brookside. While required modernizations to the pumping stations create a canopy that obscures some of the building's former architecture and the once red brick façade is now white, the original deco-era lines of the building are still visible.*
- Texaco Service Station, Sixty-second Terrace and Brookside Plaza, 1934–71. *The first of the stations to close, it started life as Fowler's Filling Station and was changed to Howell's in 1938. William Knop took over in*

This page: The façade of the former Texaco filling station at Sixty-second Terrace and Brookside Plaza is still apparent in the 2009 renovation. *Courtesy of the Kansas City (MO) Landmarks Commission and the author.*

1940, the first occasion it can be documented as a Texaco station. Robert Hennessy took over the business in 1970, the year before it closed. For one year, 1972, it operated as Log Cabin Antiques and thereafter has always been used as a restaurant. The Monastery, a uniquely styled wine bar, operated from 1973 to 1985; Joe D's followed immediately until 2008, and in 2009, it became Julian. Throughout the changes, the exterior has remained remarkably true to its original look.

- DX (Conoco) Station, 3 West 63rd Street, 1938-1982. *Duke's DX Station, operated by Archie Duke, opened in 1938. It was the last filling station to open in Brookside, and the second to close, and according to city*

This page: The former DX filling station at Sixty-third and Main is less recognizable in its present function as the Brookside Neighborhood Office. *Courtesy of the Kansas City (MO) Landmarks Commission and the author.*

directories, and was always operated by Duke. The building apparently stood vacant for a number of years, was briefly EJ Labels for less, but since 1994 has been the Brookside Neighborhood Office, a copy, printing and office supply store. An addition had been made to the east end of the property to accommodate an additional tenant. That addition significantly changed the look of the building, obscuring some of the original architecture.

Chapter 10

THE 2000S

HOME RULE

In December 2000, Miller Nichols, J.C.'s son and successor at the Nichols Company, passed away at the age of eighty-nine. While many had quibbled from time to time with the second generation's methods, there had been little doubt that, at its core, the Nichols Company still believed in the principles upon which J.C. Nichols had built the firm and the Country Club District. But now the last vestiges of the Nichols Company's *noblesse oblige* were gone. As Brookside emerged into the new century, there was ambiguity about who was in charge of Brookside's north side. The Nichols Company name was still used in the context of ownership and management, but it was a property management company that oversaw the day-to-day operations, and a new owner, Highwoods Properties, which actually owned the old Nichols properties. For some, there was a sense of insecurity about the viability of the shops.

Close eyes were trained on the Dime Store, long considered a marker of the health of Brookside. A seeming anachronism in the modern retail market, if the Dime Store remained viable, locals believed surely there was hope for the rest of the shops. But another longtime Brookside fixture, the Book Shop in Brookside, closed in February 2000. Yes, there had been property management concerns, but the owners, Roy Beaty and Deborah Cramer, cited other, more global factors in keeping their business competitive—online shopping and national bookstore chains. There had been at least one bookstore in Brookside from the beginning and at times as many as three. Now there would be none.

The notion of large retailers, often called "big-box" stores, elicited an understandable level of concern among Brookside merchants. Not only did

The sign comes down on the last Milgram's grocery store in Kansas City, 2003. *Courtesy of the author.*

such stores' tendency to swallow markets whole pose a threat to individual shops, but they also posed a threat to the physical character of Brookside. Many merchants and some in the media questioned whether new owner Highwoods's struggles to manage Brookside whispered of an intent to replace Brookside with big-box stores, an almost certain death knell for Brookside's old-fashioned tradition of locally owned and operated businesses. Everyone wondered if there was anything that could be done to stop such a formidable threat.

LOCALLY OWNED: BKS REAL ESTATE

It wasn't long after Highwoods Properties purchased the Nichols Company in the late 1990s that it began to divest itself of some of its assets. In 1999, Highwoods announced that several commercial properties were up for sale, including Brookside neighbors the Colonial, Crestwood and Romanelli Shops. True, many merchants in all these areas weren't happy with the current management situation, but Highwoods was still, as the saying goes, the devil they knew. The prospect of selling these properties yet again, so soon, made the future seem too vague.

Then came a glimmer of hope. The merchants in Crestwood banded together to buy that center. The purchase price wasn't confirmed, but speculation was that it was about $2 million. The sale showed a willingness on Highwoods's part to consider local bids, not just those from other large, national developers. In Brookside, rumors swirled amid raised expectations and dashed hopes for the next two years. The muddle did not significantly undermine confidence in the area, however. A review of Brookside store openings and closures during the period shows what is effectively a wash—for every store that left, another came. None—so far, Brookside merchants said with held breath—was of the unwanted national chain variety.

So when a rumor of a buyer for Brookside—and a local one at that— surfaced in 2003, it was hard for the Brookside community to believe too quickly. The potential buyer turned out to be one that had recently purchased another former Nichols property, the Red Bridge Shopping Center. The point man for the investors, local real estate developer and manager George Gilchrist, was a former Brookside resident. Tenants in Red Bridge seemed

After years of vacancy, BKS Real Estate renovated the former Standard Oil Station as one of its first projects after buying the former Nichols Company properties in 2000. *Courtesy of the Brookside Business Association.*

pleased with the new ownership so far, calling Gilchrist's firm hands-on and already more of a day-to-day presence than Highwoods had been.

The Brookside deal was announced in October 2003 and closed in January 2004. Gilchrist was only one of a number of investors on the deal that incorporated as BKS Real Estate. "BKS" had long been an acronym for all things Brookside, so the name had a familiar feel to it. The *Kansas City Star* reported the price tag as an estimated $15 million. Almost immediately, BKS Real Estate announced projects that gave Brooksiders reason to feel confidence they hadn't enjoyed in some time. In particular, the grocery store long owned by the Meiners family would be purchased by another Kansas City grocery store family institution, Cosentino's. The Amoco station at Sixty-second Terrace was transformed into the Roasterie Café, the retail outlet of Brookside entrepreneur and so-called "Bean Baron" Danny O'Neill, who had made his Roasterie coffee brand a regional force. The Milgram's store, which had flagged in reputation over the last few years, would be renovated as a new Price Chopper, another trusted local name.

For the first time in a long time, confidence in Brookside was on the rise. But those working within the organization were continuing plans to make certain—as much as certain can be made—that regardless of how the BKS Real Estate ownership worked out, Brookside would remain intact forever.

PUBLIC POLICY AT WORK: THE OVERLAY DISTRICT AND THE CID

In 1998, when the Brookside Business Association contracted with the Southtown Council for management, it forged what had been a friendly relationship of many years into a formidable partnership. The Southtown Council's bailiwick was the business, institutional and neighborhood community east and south of Brookside, areas that had faced considerable issues over the last twenty years. Business loss, real and perceived issues of safety and crumbling infrastructure were the sorts of problems with which Southtown had become adept at dealing. In particular, it enjoyed a strong reputation among public officials at city hall. Southtown's executive director, Marti Lee, was known as an energetic and tireless advocate for the area and a first-class problem solver.

In 2000, City Councilman Jim Rowland, whose district included Brookside, initiated efforts at the city to create a special zoning overlay district for Brookside, one designed to limit the ability of national retailers

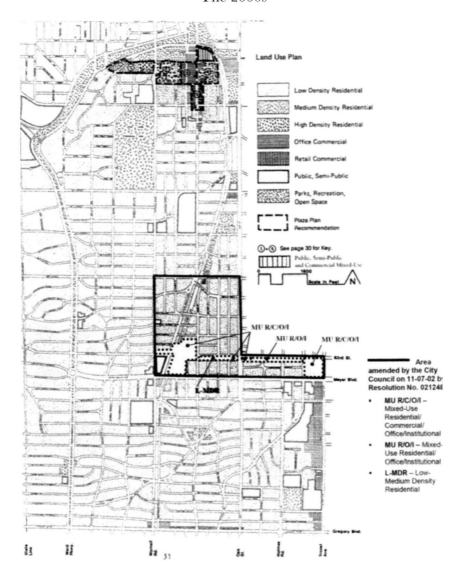

The City of Kansas City, Missouri, enacted ordinances to restrict the size of development in Brookside and along Sixty-third Street to the east. *Courtesy of the Kansas City (MO) Department of Planning and Development.*

and big-box stores to make Brookside a location. With its new management, the Brookside Business Association took advantage of that leverage and went to work, meeting with neighborhoods, businesses and property owners in the area, including Highwoods Properties. Everyone wondered how Highwoods would react to zoning changes that might hamper its ability to market the Brookside properties. But Highwoods supported the idea of the overlay district. The firm issued statements saying that it wanted to support the measures that would preserve the character of Brookside. Its cooperation was a pleasant surprise and made the initiative much easier. The overlay district was quickly adopted by council.

Rather than prohibit the category of businesses that had locals concerned, the Brookside ordinance set out to exclude many of the characteristics of such businesses. Limits were put on the amount of parking dedicated to any one business (typically calculated in relationship to building size). Certain types of lighting and building heights were restricted. Building alterations to accommodate multiple businesses (listed specifically on a menu of business types) were prohibited. The overlay district, officially called District BBD (Brookside Business District) in the city's zoning ordinance, wasn't confined to the traditional Brookside Shops boundaries. It extended east along the south side of Sixty-third Street all the way to Troost Avenue. The ordinance hadn't simply prevented big-box development in Brookside—it had made certain any big-box competition was kept at arms' distance. The ordinance was a victory for the association, but there was still work to be done, and the next step would require considerably more effort.

In 1997, the State of Missouri passed a Community Improvement District (CID) Act, enabling local areas to establish themselves as public entities, albeit subordinate to the city in which they exist. As public entities, CIDs would have the authority to levy additional property assessments and sales tax. For Brookside, this meant a funding mechanism for public improvements. The tool was ideally suited for Brookside, with its small, self-contained geography and a small number of property owners. The Brookside Business Association saw it as the perfect way to gain continuity between the properties north and south of Sixty-third Street. Businesses on the north, under the ownership of first the Nichols Company and then Highwoods Properties, enjoyed a high and consistent level of services, including on-site security, regular snow removal and maintenance and improvements to the surroundings. On the south side, where there were multiple owners, there was no such consistency. Under a CID, all properties could enjoy the same level of service.

The sticking point in the CID concept was that both the majority of the number of owners and the owners representing the majority of the total property values had to agree. In either case, forming a CID would mean the involvement of the Nichols Company. There, the Brookside Business Association met with opposition. The Nicholas Company claimed that the

CID offered it no benefit, as it was already providing services to its tenants and maintenance to its property. Since this was also the period when the company was entertaining potential buyers, it may have seen the CID formation as a move that could make the property a less attractive purchase. Regardless, before discussions concluded, the properties belonged to Highwoods, which shared the Nichols Company's apathy for the idea. It may have supported the zoning changes, but not this. The CID idea languished.

When BKS Real Estate bought the property, the association was surprised to find the new owners were supportive of the CID concept. It saw the benefits of the plan that would bring uniformity to the area, thereby improving the value of its property. With its support, the CID effort moved forward. Fraught with regulatory requirements, it would be 2005 before the Brookside Community Improvement District was formed and another year or so before the revenue stream generated enough to begin projects. Since that time, however, Brookside has seen dramatic improvements. Some—like

Formation of the Brookside Community Improvement District makes it possible for the area to continue to invest in enhancements, like its contribution to the renovation of Brookside Court Park at Sixty-third Street and Brookside Boulevard. *Courtesy of the author.*

landscaping, parking lot upgrades, litter control and comprehensive security patrol—are noticeable by merchants and patrons alike. Others—like snow removal, coordinated trash collection for the businesses and changes to the management of events and promotion—are less apparent. Funding from the CID has also permitted Brookside to create a long-range plan, allowing for a more strategic approach to anticipating improvements and planning for contingencies. After five years of operation, the success of the Brookside Community Improvement District, combined with earlier steps like the move to professional management of the association and the overlay district, have laid a strong foundation for Brookside's long-term health, just as it approaches the end of its first one hundred years.

CATALOGUE: BROOKSIDE'S OLDEST BUSINESSES

As Brookside approaches the century mark, it has both witnessed and reflected the changes in its neighborhoods, in the city and in national shifts in how and where we shop. Yet what is most often cited as Brookside's inherent charm are those ways in which it has never changed—its ties to the neighborhoods, the appeal of its old buildings and the familiar names above the awnings. Each decade has seen one or two shops appear that have remained a part of Brookside through the years, providing a sort of living time capsule to all the eras of Brookside's great history. Some have changed hands, updated their name, moved to a different Brookside address or tweaked their merchandising, but they remain quintessentially "Brookside." The following is the List of Twenty-one—twenty-one businesses that, at the close of the 2000s, have been in Brookside for twenty-one years or more.

- Foo's Fabulous Frozen Custard—6235 Brookside Plaza, 1989.
- Brookside Real Estate—9 West Sixty-third Street, 1987.
- Express Photo—6310 Main Street, 1986.
- Commerce Bank—6336 Brookside Plaza, 1985.
- Brooksider Bar & Grill—6330 Brookside Plaza, 1985.
- Drs. Martin and Deborah Isenberg—6274 Brookside Boulevard, 1982.
- Charlie Hooper's Bar & Grill—12 West Sixty-third Street, 1980.
- Hallmark Shop—6245 Brookside Boulevard, 1979.
- Hank of Hair—6315 Brookside Plaza, 1977.
- Noah's Ark Veterinary Clinic—6305 Main Street, 1971.

The popularity of its annual summer Sidewalk Sale is just one demonstration of the continuing viability of the Brookside Shops. *Courtesy of the author.*

- Baskin-Robbins Ice Cream—336 West Sixty-third Street, 1964.
- Rydell Tailors—6231 Brookside Boulevard, 1952.
- Brookside Shoe Repair—6247 Brookside Plaza, 1948.
- Brookside Toy & Science—330 West Sixty-third Street, 1948.
- Jacobs Properties—6315 Brookside Plaza, 1938.
- Shop Beautiful—320 West Sixty-third Street, 1936.
- Hodge Family Dentistry—6247 Brookside Boulevard, 1934.
- Brookside Barber Shop—308 West Sixty-third Street, 1930.
- Brookside 66 Service Station—6244 Main Street, 1928.
- U.S. Post Office, Country Club Station—108 West Sixty-third Street, 1925.
- Drummond Cleaners—6328 Brookside Plaza, 1919.

BIBLIOGRAPHY

The following books provided both detail on Brookside history and the larger context for understanding Brookside's place in local and national history.

Dodd, Monroe. *A Splendid Ride: The Streetcars of Kansas City 1870–1950.* Kansas City, MO: Kansas City Star Books, 2002.

Garwood, Darrell. *Crossroads of America: The Story of Kansas City.* New York: W.W. Norton & Company, Inc., 1948.

Haskell, Henry C., Jr., and Richard B. Fowler. *City of the Future: The Story of Kansas City 1850–1950.* Kansas City, MO: Frank Glenn Publishing Co., Inc., 1950.

Jacobs, Harry. *The Road from Rags to Riches: An American Dream.* N.p.: self-published, 1976.

Liston, Helen. *The Dime Store.* N.p.: self-published, 2002.

McAlester, Virginia, and Lee McAlester. *A Field Guide to American Houses.* New York: Alfred A. Knopf, 1986.

Montgomery, Rick, and Shiel Kasper. *Kansas City: An American Story.* Kansas City, MO: Kansas City Star Books, 1999.

Pearson, Robert, and Brad Pearson. *The J.C. Nichols Chronicle*. Kansas City, MO: Country Club Plaza Press, 1994.

Urban Land Institute. *The Community Builders Handbook*. Washington, D.C.: Urban Land Institute, reprint 2000.

Worley, William S. *J.C. Nichols and the Shaping of Kansas City*. Columbia and London: University of Missouri Press, 1990.

ABOUT THE AUTHOR

For the last thirty years, LaDene Morton has lived and worked in the Brookside area, including ten years as a tenant in Brookside and later serving as project manager to the Brookside Community Improvement District. For those same thirty years, she has worked in the field of community development research and analysis and spent her career studying how communities like Brookside work. In addition, her historical novel, *What Lies West*, was a 2010 finalist for the WILLA Literary Award, presented by the writers' association Women Writing the West.

Photo by Don Wolfe.

Visit us at
www.historypress.net